Blessings to you
Shui & Dowsing
this blessed year of the Rat!

Love you!
your Soul
Sister

Debbie

FENG SHUI

FOR

2020

THE YEAR OF THE METAL RAT

鼠年運程下卷

庚子

INDEX

PREFACE

With the recent wave of Feng Shui Renaissance, we found ourselves once again drenched in a newfound interest and respect for the historic art and science of Classical Feng Shui.

If you're a careful observer, you can certainly observe what this new wave of Feng Shui pushed in: an era of accessibility where F-I-Y or "Feng Shui-It Yourself" methods emerge ubiquitously left, right and centre. Everywhere, Feng Shui enthusiasts and amateurs can be seen dipping their hands and proclaiming the methods and applications to Feng Shui in ways never seen before. As a master trainer, consultant and practitioner of this field, I am of course more than glad to see this escalating trend and interests in the field of Feng Shui and its complementary studies, Chinese Astrology, Qi Men, Yi Jing and Face Reading taking off.

This book is produced as my call to answer the pressing demand from the masses seeking accessible Feng Shui information and knowledge, and as well as to provide an avenue of learning for those who for reasons of the time, or perhaps distance, are unable to attend my annual Feng Shui and Astrology seminars. Just treat this annual publication as your trusty go-to guidebook to foster a new layer of understanding on the Qi that will influence properties in 2020, and the correct know-how on how to best deploy these energies in your home and workplace to your advantage. The book you're holding also clarifies and draws a comprehensive overview for the year based on the Flying Stars chart and the Afflictions for 2020.

Together with the monthly Flying Stars outlook based on the Main Door and Bedroom locations for all Twelve Months of 2020, the section on the Flying Stars for all 8 Houses for 2020 presents a clean and solid foundation to enable you to gain a more direct and encompassing insights on how the Qi in 2020 will affect you and your family, or your business.

If you're unfamiliar with the methods of plotting a Flying Stars chart, don't worry, I'll make it more convenient for you. Just go to the link as indicated on Page 12 to obtain your individual access code and generate your own results with the online Flying Stars calculator there.

Those with a more thorough understanding of Chinese Metaphysics studies would know that luck is divided into Man Luck, Earth Luck and Heaven Luck - all collectively known as the Cosmic Trinity. Notably, Feng Shui makes up only one single component of the

Cosmic Trinity, so don't be exceedingly concerned if there is a presence of negative stars in your property. Remember, any view in Feng Shui is incomplete without taking into consideration the proportion and the bigger picture of the situations or structures. Hence, the full impact of the stars must also be viewed in light of the landforms in the surrounding area, which will trigger or activate the stars' negative or positive energies.

If you're interested and would like to know more about how to do simple assessments of forms, you may want to look into my Feng Shui for Homebuyers series.

Every once in a while, I would give some "words of wisdom" to my clients to let them view things in a bigger picture. Giving in to your fear and paranoia will succumb you to a state of inaction and thus, making you incapable of accepting changes. It is important for you to note that in Chinese Metaphysics, nothing is completely bad or purely good. For every Yin, there's a Yang, and vice versa. Worrying is essentially useless; the most important thing you need to do is to understand what the Feng Shui influences are, prioritise your actions and make informed decisions.

I hope you'll find this book supportive, practical and most importantly, informative. To wrap it up, I wish you a smooth sailing year ahead in the Year of the Metal Rat!

Warmest regards,

Dato' Joey Yap
July 2019

Connect with us:

www.joeyyap.com   **JOEYYAP TV** www.youtube/joeyyap

f @DatoJoeyYap   @RealJoeyYap   @JoeyYap

Academy website:
www.masteryacademy.com | jya.masteryacademy.com | www.baziprofiling.com

Exclusive content available for download with your purchase of the Feng Shui for 2020 book.

Claim your FREE ONLINE ACCESS now at:
www.masteryacademy.com/bookbonus2020

BONUS CONTENT

FREE
DOWNLOAD

FSR93BC8

Expires
31st December 2020

Introduction

Introduction

In order to fully utilise the information and material in this book, you need to have a basic understanding of how to derive certain information - for example, the location of your Main Door, the various directional sectors in your home and your personal Gua Number.

How to ascertain the Location of your Main Door

In order to tap into the beneficial Qi of the year and the kind of Qi that will influence your home in 2020, it is important to be able to identify the various directional sectors of your home and also determine which sector your Main Door is located. This knowledge is particularly important for those who wish to make use of the information contained in the Eight Houses for 2020 chapter, which is based on the directional sector in where your house or office's Main Door is found.

The first step is to divide your house into Nine Grids. To do this, you just need a simple scout's compass and the plan of your house. On the plan of your house, draw the Nine Grids as illustrated in Step 1 and Step 2.

Step 1

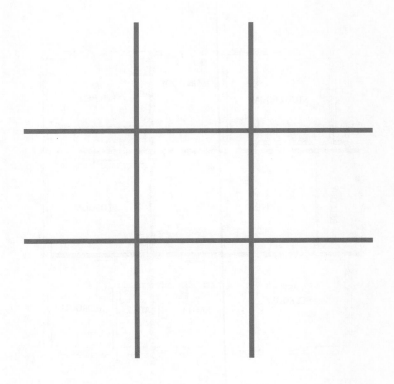

Step 2

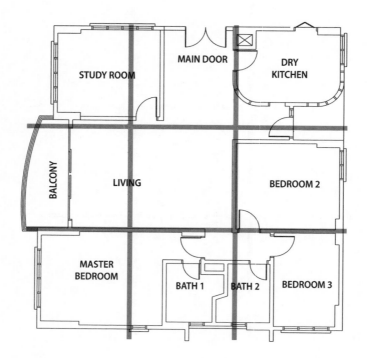

Next, stand at the center point of your house and establish the North direction using the compass. On the plan of your house, mark out the sector in that direction as North and then identify all the other directions according to the directions of the compass.

Step 3

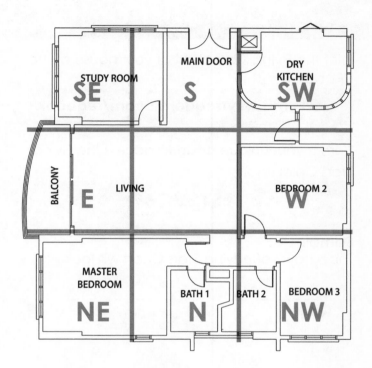

Using this simple Nine Grids, you will be able to identify the favourable and unfavourable sectors of your home and make less or more use of the corresponding rooms. You will also be able to ascertain the location of your Main Door and determine what kind of energies will influence your home in 2020.

Flying Stars Feng Shui Calculator

Print the Flying Stars chart of your house at the URL below:

www.masteryacademy.com/regbook

Here is your unique code to access the Flying Stars Calculator:

FS12VC69

Sample:
This is how your Flying Stars Chart will look like:

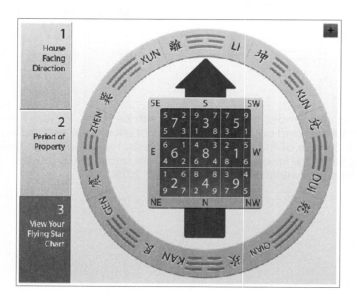

Find Your Gua Number and Animal Sign

Gua Numbers for Years 1912 - 2007

年 - The Year of the Metal Rat

Year of Birth		Male	Female
1912 壬子 Ren Zi	Water Rat	7	8
1913 癸丑 Gui Chou	Water Ox	6	9
1914 甲寅 Jia Yin	Wood Tiger	2	1
1915 乙卯 Yi Mao	Wood Rabbit	4	2
1916 丙辰 Bing Chen	Fire Dragon	3	3
1917 丁巳 Ding Si	Fire Snake	2	4
1918 戊午 Wu Wu	Earth Horse	1	8
1919 己未 Ji Wei	Earth Goat	9	6
1920 庚申 Geng Shen	Metal Monkey	8	7
1921 辛酉 Xin You	Metal Rooster	7	8
1922 壬戌 Ren Xu	Water Dog	6	9
1923 癸亥 Gui Hai	Water Pig	2	1
1924 甲子 Jia Zi	Wood Rat	4	2
1925 乙丑 Yi Chou	Wood Ox	3	3
1926 丙寅 Bing Yin	Fire Tiger	2	4
1927 丁卯 Ding Mao	Fire Rabbit	1	8
1928 戊辰 Wu Chen	Earth Dragon	9	6
1929 己巳 Ji Si	Earth Snake	8	7
1930 庚午 Geng Wu	Metal Horse	7	8
1931 辛未 Xin Wei	Metal Goat	6	9
1932 壬申 Ren Shen	Water Monkey	2	1
1933 癸酉 Gui You	Water Rooster	4	2
1934 甲戌 Jia Xu	Wood Dog	3	3
1935 乙亥 Yi Hai	Wood Pig	2	4

Year of Birth		Male	Female
1936 丙子 Bing Zi	Fire Rat	1	8
1937 丁丑 Ding Chou	Fire Ox	9	6
1938 戊寅 Wu Yin	Earth Tiger	8	7
1939 己卯 Ji Mao	Earth Rabbit	7	8
1940 庚辰 Geng Chen	Metal Dragon	6	9
1941 辛巳 Xin Si	Metal Snake	2	1
1942 壬午 Ren Wu	Water Horse	4	2
1943 癸未 Gui Wei	Water Goat	3	3
1944 甲申 Jia Shen	Wood Monkey	2	4
1945 乙酉 Yi You	Wood Rooster	1	8
1946 丙戌 Bing Xu	Fire Dog	9	6
1947 丁亥 Ding Hai	Fire Pig	8	7
1948 戊子 Wu Zi	Earth Rat	7	8
1949 己丑 Ji Chou	Earth Ox	6	9
1950 庚寅 Geng Yin	Metal Tiger	2	1
1951 辛卯 Xin Mao	Metal Rabbit	4	2
1952 壬辰 Ren Chen	Water Dragon	3	3
1953 癸巳 Gui Si	Water Snake	2	4
1954 甲午 Jia Wu	Wood Horse	1	8
1955 乙未 Yi Wei	Wood Goat	9	6
1956 丙申 Bing Shen	Fire Monkey	8	7
1957 丁酉 Ding You	Fire Rooster	7	8
1958 戊戌 Wu Xu	Earth Dog	6	9
1959 己亥 Ji Hai	Earth Pig	2	1

Year of Birth		Male	Female
1960 庚子 Geng Zi	Metal Rat	4	2
1961 辛丑 Xin Chou	Metal Ox	3	3
1962 壬寅 Ren Yin	Water Tiger	2	4
1963 癸卯 Gui Mao	Water Rabbit	1	8
1964 甲辰 Jia Chen	Wood Dragon	9	6
1965 乙巳 Yi Si	Wood Snake	8	7
1966 丙午 Bing Wu	Fire Horse	7	8
1967 丁未 Ding Wei	Fire Goat	6	9
1968 戊申 Wu Shen	Earth Monkey	2	1
1969 己酉 Ji You	Earth Rooster	4	2
1970 庚戌 Geng Xu	Metal Dog	3	3
1971 辛亥 Xin Hai	Metal Pig	2	4
1972 壬子 Ren Zi	Water Rat	1	8
1973 癸丑 Gui Chou	Water Ox	9	6
1974 甲寅 Jia Yin	Wood Tiger	8	7
1975 乙卯 Yi Mao	Wood Rabbit	7	8
1976 丙辰 Bing Chen	Fire Dragon	6	9
1977 丁巳 Ding Si	Fire Snake	2	1
1978 戊午 Wu Wu	Earth Horse	4	2
1979 己未 Ji Wei	Earth Goat	3	3
1980 庚申 Geng Shen	Metal Monkey	2	4
1981 辛酉 Xin You	Metal Rooster	1	8
1982 壬戌 Ren Xu	Water Dog	9	6
1983 癸亥 Gui Hai	Water Pig	8	7

Year of Birth		Male	Female
1984 甲子 Jia Zi	Wood Rat	7	8
1985 乙丑 Yi Chou	Wood Ox	6	9
1986 丙寅 Bing Yin	Fire Tiger	2	1
1987 丁卯 Ding Mao	Fire Rabbit	4	2
1988 戊辰 Wu Chen	Earth Dragon	3	3
1989 己巳 Ji Si	Earth Snake	2	4
1990 庚午 Geng Wu	Metal Horse	1	8
1991 辛未 Xin Wei	Metal Goat	9	6
1992 壬申 Ren Shen	Water Monkey	8	7
1993 癸酉 Gui You	Water Rooster	7	8
1994 甲戌 Jia Xu	Wood Dog	6	9
1995 乙亥 Yi Hai	Wood Pig	2	1
1996 丙子 Bing Zi	Fire Rat	4	2
1997 丁丑 Ding Chou	Fire Ox	3	3
1998 戊寅 Wu Yin	Earth Tiger	2	4
1999 己卯 Ji Mao	Earth Rabbit	1	8
2000 庚辰 Geng Chen	Metal Dragon	9	6
2001 辛巳 Xin Si	Metal Snake	8	7
2002 壬午 Ren Wu	Water Horse	7	8
2003 癸未 Gui Wei	Water Goat	6	9
2004 甲申 Jia Shen	Wood Monkey	2	1
2005 乙酉 Yi You	Wood Rooster	4	2
2006 丙戌 Bing Xu	Fire Dog	3	3
2007 丁亥 Ding Hai	Fire Pig	2	4

• Please note that the date for the Chinese Solar Year starts on Feb 4. This means that if you were born in Feb 2 of 2002, you belong to the previous year of 2001.

Gua Numbers for Years 2008 - 2103

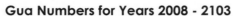

Year of Birth			Gua Number for Male	Gua Number for Female
2008	戊子 Wu Zi	Earth Rat	1	8
2009	己丑 Ji Chou	Earth Ox	9	6
2010	庚寅 Geng Yin	Metal Tiger	8	7
2011	辛卯 Xin Mao	Metal Rabbit	7	8
2012	壬辰 Ren Chen	Water Dragon	6	9
2013	癸巳 Gui Si	Water Snake	2	1
2014	甲午 Jia Wu	Wood Horse	4	2
2015	乙未 Yi Wei	Wood Goat	3	3
2016	丙申 Bing Shen	Fire Monkey	2	4
2017	丁酉 Ding You	Fire Rooster	1	8
2018	戊戌 Wu Xu	Earth Dog	9	6
2019	己亥 Ji Hai	Earth Pig	8	7
2020	庚子 Geng Zi	Metal Rat	7	8
2021	辛丑 Xin Chou	Metal Ox	6	9
2022	壬寅 Ren Yin	Water Tiger	2	1
2023	癸卯 Gui Mao	Water Rabbit	4	2
2024	甲辰 Jia Chen	Wood Dragon	3	3
2025	乙巳 Yi Si	Wood Snake	2	4
2026	丙午 Bing Wu	Fire Horse	1	8
2027	丁未 Ding Wei	Fire Goat	9	6
2028	戊申 Wu Shen	Earth Monkey	8	7
2029	己酉 Ji You	Earth Rooster	7	8
2030	庚戌 Geng Xu	Metal Dog	6	9
2031	辛亥 Xin Hai	Metal Pig	2	1

Year of Birth			Gua Number for Male	Gua Number for Female
2032	壬子 Ren Zi	Water Rat	4	2
2033	癸丑 Gui Chou	Water Ox	3	3
2034	甲寅 Jia Yin	Wood Tiger	2	4
2035	乙卯 Yi Mao	Wood Rabbit	1	8
2036	丙辰 Bing Chen	Fire Dragon	9	6
2037	丁巳 Ding Si	Fire Snake	8	7
2038	戊午 Wu Wu	Earth Horse	7	8
2039	己未 Ji Wei	Earth Goat	6	9
2040	庚申 Geng Shen	Metal Monkey	2	1
2041	辛酉 Xin You	Metal Rooster	4	2
2042	壬戌 Ren Xu	Water Dog	3	3
2043	癸亥 Gui Hai	Water Pig	2	4
2044	甲子 Jia Zi	Wood Rat	1	8
2045	乙丑 Yi Chou	Wood Ox	9	6
2046	丙寅 Bing Yin	Fire Tiger	8	7
2047	丁卯 Ding Mao	Fire Rabbit	7	8
2048	戊辰 Wu Chen	Earth Dragon	6	9
2049	己巳 Ji Si	Earth Snake	2	1
2050	庚午 Geng Wu	Metal Horse	4	2
2051	辛未 Xin Wei	Metal Goat	3	3
2052	壬申 Ren Shen	Water Monkey	2	4
2053	癸酉 Gui You	Water Rooster	1	8
2054	甲戌 Jia Xu	Wood Dog	9	6
2055	乙亥 Yi Hai	Wood Pig	8	7

Year of Birth			Gua Number for Male	Gua Number for Female
2056	丙子 Bing Zi	Fire Rat	7	8
2057	丁丑 Ding Chou	Fire Ox	6	9
2058	戊寅 Wu Yin	Earth Tiger	2	1
2059	己卯 Ji Mao	Earth Rabbit	4	2
2060	庚辰 Geng Chen	Metal Dragon	3	3
2061	辛巳 Xin Si	Metal Snake	2	4
2062	壬午 Ren Wu	Water Horse	1	8
2063	癸未 Gui Wei	Water Goat	9	6
2064	甲申 Jia Shen	Wood Monkey	8	7
2065	乙酉 Yi You	Wood Rooster	7	8
2066	丙戌 Bing Xu	Fire Dog	6	9
2067	丁亥 Ding Hai	Fire Pig	2	1
2068	戊子 Wu Zi	Earth Rat	4	2
2069	己丑 Ji Chou	Earth Ox	3	3
2070	庚寅 Geng Yin	Metal Tiger	2	4
2071	辛卯 Xin Mao	Metal Rabbit	1	8
2072	壬辰 Ren Chen	Water Dragon	9	6
2073	癸巳 Gui Si	Water Snake	8	7
2074	甲午 Jia Wu	Wood Horse	7	8
2075	乙未 Yi Wei	Wood Goat	6	9
2076	丙申 Bing Shen	Fire Monkey	2	1
2077	丁酉 Ding You	Fire Rooster	4	2
2078	戊戌 Wu Xu	Earth Dog	3	3
2079	己亥 Ji Hai	Earth Pig	2	4

Year of Birth			Gua Number for Male	Gua Number for Female
2080	庚子 Geng Zi	Metal Rat	1	8
2081	辛丑 Xin Chou	Metal Ox	9	6
2082	壬寅 Ren Yin	Water Tiger	8	7
2083	癸卯 Gui Mao	Water Rabbit	7	8
2084	甲辰 Jia Chen	Wood Dragon	6	9
2085	乙巳 Yi Si	Wood Snake	2	1
2086	丙午 Bing Wu	Fire Horse	4	2
2087	丁未 Ding Wei	Fire Goat	3	3
2088	戊申 Wu Shen	Earth Monkey	2	4
2089	己酉 Ji You	Earth Rooster	1	8
2090	庚戌 Geng Xu	Metal Dog	9	6
2091	辛亥 Xin Hai	Metal Pig	8	7
2092	壬子 Ren Zi	Water Rat	7	8
2093	癸丑 Gui Chou	Water Ox	6	9
2094	甲寅 Jia Yin	Wood Tiger	2	1
2095	乙卯 Yi Mao	Wood Rabbit	4	2
2096	丙辰 Bing Chen	Fire Dragon	3	3
2097	丁巳 Ding Si	Fire Snake	2	4
2098	戊午 Wu Wu	Earth Horse	1	8
2099	己未 Ji Wei	Earth Goat	9	6
2100	庚申 Geng Shen	Metal Monkey	8	7
2101	辛酉 Xin You	Metal Rooster	7	8
2102	壬戌 Ren Xu	Water Dog	6	9
2103	癸亥 Gui Hai	Water Pig	2	1

• Please note that the date for the Chinese Solar Year starts on Feb 4. This means that if you were born in Feb 2 of 2002, you belong to the previous year of 2001.

Using the 12-Month Outlook based on Bedroom Location Section

To use this section, you must know the location of your property's Main Door and the location of your bedroom. Note that your bedroom may be located on the Ground Floor or 1st or 2nd floor.

1. Identify the location of your Main Door.

In the example below, the Main Door is located in the West. So turn to page 153, for the section on the 12-month outlook for all 8 bedrooms for a West Sector Main Door.

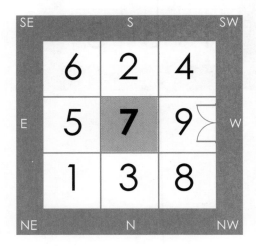

2. Identify the location of your bedroom.

In the example below, the bedroom is located in the South. So turn to page 162 and you will find the 12-month outlook for your bedroom, located in a West Sector Main Door.

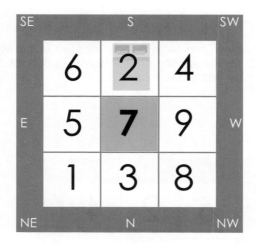

2020 Feng Shui Afflictions

2020 Feng Shui Afflictions

The Three Killings (三煞) – SOUTH 157.6° - 202.5°

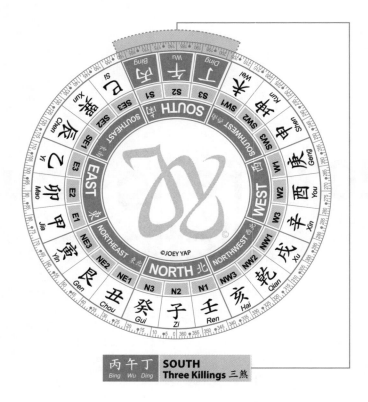

| 丙 午 丁 | **SOUTH** |
| Bing Wu Ding | **Three Killings** 三煞 |

This year, the Three Killings is in the South sector. This area should preferably be left alone and remain undisturbed throughout the year, but it should especially not be activated for groundbreaking or renovations. Otherwise, you may risk causing some serious negative consequences for the property itself, and its inhabitants. Potential repercussions include mishaps and accidents, robberies, theft, loss of wealth and material possessions, as well as persistent health troubles and complications.

The Five Yellow (五黃) – EAST 67.6° - 112.5°

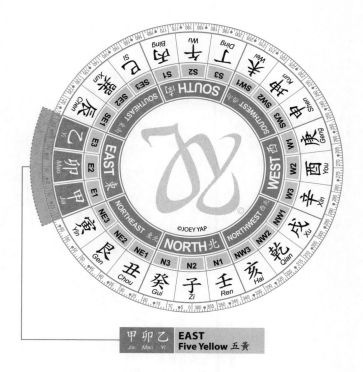

甲 卯 乙	EAST
Jia Mao Yi	Five Yellow 五黃

The Five Yellow Star is present in the East sector for the year 2020. As this Star has extremely volatile and negative energies, this sector should preferably be avoided for major use throughout the year. If it is impossible to avoid using this area, then it would be best to try to neutralise the negative energies of the Five Yellow Star by using more metal items in the area; preferably those made of brass, copper, and iron. If your property faces the East direction, it is advisable to hold off on all planned renovations until the next year. However, if this is unavoidable, then one should only begin on the renovation procedure after suitably and carefully selecting a good date for it.

The Year Breaker (歲破) – SOUTH 2 172.6° - 187.5°

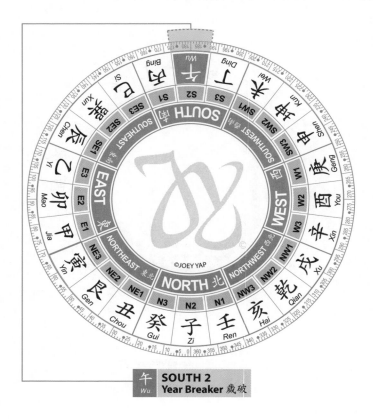

| 午 Wu | **SOUTH 2** **Year Breaker** 歲破 |

The Year Breaker Star flies into the South 2 sector for the year. It would be best to avoid all forms of renovation or groundbreaking works in this sector to avoid incurring any negative consequences. The Year Breaker is also sometimes referred to as the 'Wrath of the Grand Duke.' Disturbing the Year Breaker or aggravating it in any way may lead to serious repercussions with outcomes that could be worse than the ones triggered by the Grand Duke.

The Grand Duke (太歲) – NORTH 2 352.6° - 7.5°

子 **NORTH 2**
Zi **Grand Duke 太歲**

In 2020, the Grand Duke flies into the North 2 sector of your property. Avoid aggravating the negative energies of this star by disturbing this sector, either through renovation or groundbreaking. Potential accidents and catastrophes are likely if the Grand Duke is activated, and there are also serious implications of medical problems. It would not be good to face the North 2 direction during work, or even during major work discussions, and meetings. It would be best to try to put your back to this direction, as that will enable you to regain the upper hand in professional negotiations and in all career-related activities and projects.

Flying Stars Feng Shui for 2020

Flying Stars Feng Shui for 2020

Overview

Wealth Sectors   : Northwest, West

Academic Sectors: Southwest, Northeast

Negative Sectors   : East, South

2020 Flying Stars by Sectors

Direction/ Location	Annual Star	Forecast
東南 Southeast	六白 6 White	In the Southeast sector for 2020, the presence of the #6 White Star suggests the possibility of making strides in the office and ascending the career ladder. There is a likelihood of being recognised for one's own efforts. It would be good to use the Southeast sector if you wish to make more of an impact at the workplace or in your career. Using a Southeast door from which you enter your office can also help boost your influence at work and your network of professional acquaintances. But while the #6 White is generally benevolent, if activated by negative forms it can lead to sudden, unexpected changes in the workplace, and possible medical complications to the kidneys and legs.
南 South	二黑 2 Black	The #2 Black flies into the South sector for 2020, so it would be best to avoid using this area as much as possible throughout the year. The negative influences of this Star can bring about persistent illnesses and health troubles. Where possible, pregnant women should completely avoid using the South sector. It also bodes well for gains and investment through the property and real estate industries. It can also bring about stomach and digestive problems. If avoiding usage of the South is not completely possible, then it is possible to weaken the negative Qi in the sector by placing metal objects of brass, copper, bronze, or pewter in the area.

2020 Flying Stars by Sectors

Direction/ Location	Annual Star	Forecast
西南 Southwest	四綠 4 Green	The #4 Green bodes well for academic, scholarly pursuits, and those who use this sector will find themselves excelling in their studies. Writers and people who are involved in academic and research work will benefit greatly from using the Southwest sector, and the effects will be evident in the work they produce. This #4 Green also bodes well for romance and love, and couples that use this sector will enjoy better a better relationship. If you use a Southwest Main Door, or sit in the Southwest sector of your office, you are likely to do quite a bit of travelling during the year.
西 West	九紫 9 Purple	The effects of the #9 Purple in the West sector suggest potential success through the demonstration of one's talents and capabilities. You will benefit greatly from expressing your skills and attributes. However, there is the likelihood of suffering from depression and some form of emotional instability.

2020 Flying Stars by Sectors

Direction/ Location	Annual Star	Forecast
西北 Northwest	八白 8 White	This sector would be the one to look out for if you are seeking prosperity and good fortune. Having your Main Door located in this sector would be especially beneficial as it will help usher in positive energies, which in turn will bring about great returns in the form of investments. The #8 White is also excellent for encouraging a career boost and enhancing one's reputation. If the Main Door is not found in this sector, you can still harness its benefits by activating it with water features.
北 North	三碧 3 Jade	The #3 Jade Star flies into the North sector for the year, and you should try to avoid using or activating this sector as much as possible, or otherwise quarrels and arguments are the likely result. Tensions will run high, with some of the more extreme consequences of the #3 Jade resulting in legal problems and tensions. The effects of the #3 Jade can be countered and lessened somewhat by placing an oil lamp in this sector for the duration of 2020.

2020 Flying Stars by Sectors

Direction/ Location	Annual Star	Forecast
東北 Northeast	一白 1 White	Where possible, consider using a Northeast Main Door or entrance door for the year of 2020. The #1 White in the Northeast sector indicates the possibility of fresh beginnings and new ventures and projects. Couples who are keen to tie the knot or start a family will bode well to use this sector. The #1 White can also lead to good name and reputation, and bring about nobility. However, depression and emotional instability can also be a potential problem.
東 East	五黃 5 Yellow	The East is the most dangerous sector for the year of 2020. It would be best to avoid all major and important activities in this sector of your home or business, as the negative consequences can otherwise be bad. Avoid renovating the area, or groundbreaking. When this sector is activated, it could lead to possible accidents, disasters, and catastrophes. It is best to keep this area inactive or refrain from using it for extended periods of time. But if left with no choice but to use this area, neutralise the negative energies of the #5 Yellow by placing metal objects in the area made of brass, copper, or iron.

The Eight Types of Houses in 2020

North Sector Main Door

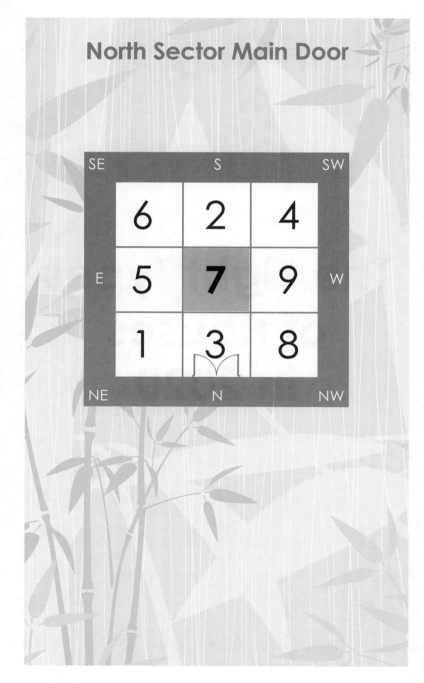

Overview

Everyone wants to feel loved, but if lovey-dovey feelings are what you're after, you won't be able to maintain those feelings for long periods of time with the presence of the Three Jade Star.

Its gloomy nature in the North sector is able to disrupt the harmony of every relationship you have with others. While it may sound upsetting and can definitely cause you to be constantly misunderstood or falsely accused, don't let its presence worry you too much.

It's time to think back about the good memories that happened in your life and feel utmost appreciation for each and every one of them because even though your relationships are not meant to flourish with the presence of this star in the North sector, it is a good idea to keep your mind focused on positive moments. The energy will help you navigate through all of the negativity that this star brings.

And although it is recommended for you to place an oil or bright red lamp in this sector to pacify its ill effects, it is best to completely ignore this sector if you want to avoid disagreements, arguments and legal problems.

It's also better if you make an effort to record all of the positivity that you have experienced throughout the year in a Gratitude Journal. Let it remind you of how blessed you truly are and help you exude more loving energy from the inside out.

If you consistently vibrate positivity through your thoughts, feelings and actions, it will be easier for you to attract positive experiences. Instead of approaching negative matters with anger, learn to be more understanding by putting yourself into other people's shoes before pointing fingers, being aware of the karma that you are creating, transforming the type of energy that you are projecting and at the same time, minimising this sector's negative energies. Having this knowledge will be able to help you handle any negative situation with ease.

Northwest Sector Main Door

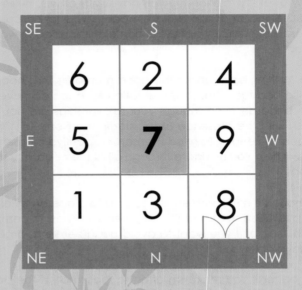

Overview

Abundance and prosperity is your birthright. If you tap into the limitless, infinite wealth energy that the Northwest sector brings in this year, you will enjoy more of its beneficial flow.

The good news is that you won't have to lift a finger if your Main Door is located in this sector. Abundance and prosperity will just flow into your life continuously and effortlessly.

Its effects will be seen in every area of your life especially your finances, but money is not the only form of abundance that will show up in your life. Apart from that, the energy of this star will also cause you to experience success in your career that will come in the form of a promotion or a salary increment.

If you've been thinking of ways to invest your money, you shouldn't think twice when you are facing this direction because you will experience an explosion of abundance. When this happens, it is important for you to remain humble. Although this is a time when you'll shine and get the recognition you've always been longing for, don't forget that many people out there are struggling. They don't have a roof over their heads or find it difficult to even eat three meals a day. Be thankful to a higher power that you are living the life of your dreams and help others who are less fortunate. Live this life by constantly being a blessing to yourself and others. Always strive to make a positive difference.

If your Main Door is not located in this sector, you can still welcome this high quality energy into your life by activating it through the placement of water features. Another way to activate it is by hanging out at this sector on a daily basis. Alternatively, you can place Yang-natured objects such as clocks, fans and televisions to bring out its natural uplifting energy.

West Sector Main Door

SE	S	SW
6	2	4
5 (E)	**7**	9 (W)
1	3	8
NE	N	NW

Overview

The West sector is home to the Nine Purple star this year. This calls for a celebration because if you position yourself towards this sector, your life will transform in positive ways.

The Nine purple's bountiful effect will cause you to be busy with to-do lists that will make you extremely happy because not only will your finances improve, the connections you have with others will be far better than before.

Basically, this sector is meant to yield thrilling, positive outcomes in anything you decide to do and since the Nine Purple star is strongly linked to getting prosperity that is permanent or long-term in nature, expect to see its influence in many areas of your life.

If you are in the creative industry, you have the potential to shine like a star. If you have been longing for an increase in salary from your boss, you will most likely get it. If you want to get married, there are high chances that you will find a suitable partner. The list of positive aspects goes on and on, but what's certain is, everything will be unfolding positively in your life if you tap into the good energy that this star brings.

So, what are you waiting for? Apply for that job that you've always wanted or start that business you've been longing for! Don't worry, you have the positive energy of the Nine Purple star to support you in all of your endeavours!

Artistic occupants of this sector will experience a surge in energy and creativity. Basically, they will be able to display more of their talents that will lead to recognition and fame.

Those planning to get married will also see their goals coming to fruition.

Basically, you can look forward to a happy and fulfilling life this year if you use this sector to your advantage.

West Sector Main Door

Southwest Sector Main Door

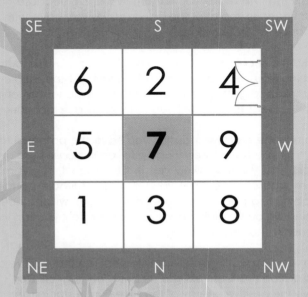

SE	S	SW
6	2	4
5	**7**	9
1	3	8
NE	N	NW

(E on the left middle, W on the right middle)

Overview

The Four Green star with its potent good luck energy resides in the Southwest sector this year.

It is the type of auspicious energy that is able to help you realise your goals and make your dreams come true. It has the ability to help artists create masterpieces, writers to produce award-winning articles and students to achieve high marks in their exams.

To experience the benefits that are present in this sector, it is best to carry out activities here. It is better if you transform the space in this sector into a study room or a bedroom. That way, more of its positivity will be stirred up to further boost your luck.

It's also a good place for you to find inspiration to get your creative juices flowing. Perhaps you are keen on painting a beautiful scenery or have pondered on the thought of carving a piece of wood statue? Go ahead and do it because nothing bad can come out of using this sector.

If your Main Door is in the Southwest, you will have more reasons to feel happy as more positive experiences will show up in your life. This particular combination will also open doors for you to travel and see the world. If you have been dying to visit a particular country, you might have a chance to do it this year! Positive outcomes will be pouring out from this direction as well. You'll be beaming with joy during your trip and come back renewed and refreshed.

This positive momentum will fortunately continue to snowball into your relationships. This is definitely a good year for you to expect more hugs and kisses from your loved ones because your bond with them is now growing stronger than ever.

South Sector Main Door

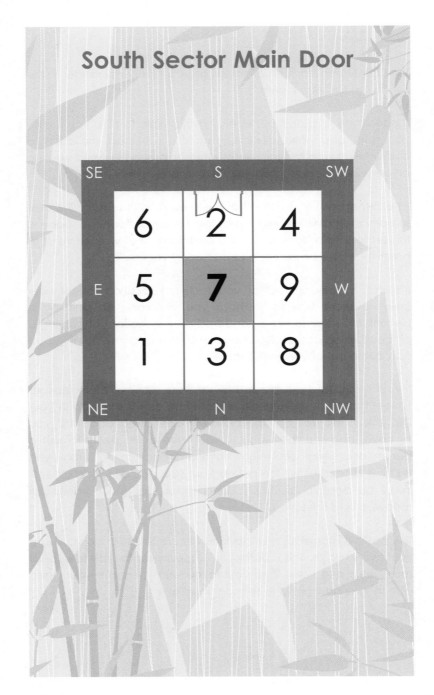

SE	S	SW
6	2	4
E 5	**7**	9 W
1	3	8
NE	N	NW

Overview

Let's face it, nobody wants to have health issues on a continuous basis. Everyone wants to enjoy life to the fullest. The worst part of having financial wealth is not being able to savour it. What's the use of having a lot of money if you're sick in bed?

Well, the Two Black which is also known as the star of sickness reminds us how valuable our health is. It exists to steer us in the right direction where health is concerned. If you are suffering from an illness, you should not freak out or worry excessively about it. Try to focus on a healthy diet, take your medications as instructed by a doctor and exercise on a regular basis.

Take an even wiser approach and avoid the South sector where the Two Black star resides. If your Main Door is located in this sector, you might want to consider moving to another house or at least, temporarily relocate to a new residence.

Otherwise, your life this year will be full of health issues and if you are already sick, it can make your current health condition be even worse. It's also a no-go zone for pregnant ladies.

If you have to use this sector, it's best to pacify its ill effects by placing a metal made out of iron, bronze, copper, pewter or brass.

And although the presence of the Two Black star sounds terrifying, it is not an entirely negative star. In fact, it is auspicious for those in the real estate industry. It also brings good luck to those dealing with investments. Expect money to flow in through these doors this year.

You will even have a chance to reap the benefit of the Two Black's positive side if you have a Bright Hall outside of your Main Door that is free from any negative features.

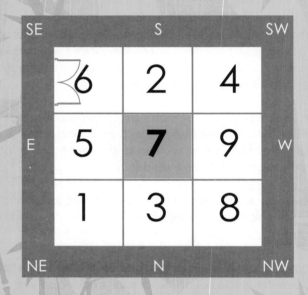

Southeast Sector Main Door

SE	S	SW
6	2	4
5 (E)	**7**	9 (W)
1	3	8
NE	N	NW

Overview

The Six White star has tremendous energy that is able to connect you to rewards, recognition and career progression if you occupy the Southeast sector this year.

Its positive energy would be amplified if your Main Door is in this location. There is high chance for you to bask in the ambience of the star's high quality energy if you have been putting in effort at your workplace. You'll be able to enjoy the fruits of your labour in the form of a salary increment.

If a promotion was beyond your reach last year, tapping into the energy of this sector will allow you to achieve it easily this year. The power and authority that this star brings will enable you to be rewarded by your superiors.

But when you hear news that you are entitled for a promotion, don't be proud and think you're all that. It's important to acknowledge the fact that you did not achieve this success on your own. Remain humble and be the type of person that continuously acquires new skills and knowledge on a regular basis. Keep positive people in your sphere of influence and let their positive traits rub off on you.

Although this sector is mostly beneficial to those in the tourism, printing and freight-related businesses, and is particularly auspicious for those in the military, academic or sports industry, anyone who uses it will be pleased with how their life will unfold.

Don't let the unwanted side-effects scare you. They will only be prevalent if negative features exist in this sector, causing problems in your workplace and health complications especially involving the legs or kidneys. Otherwise, success will be following you everywhere you go and the good energy will continuously lead you to great opportunities that already have your name written all over them.

East Sector Main Door

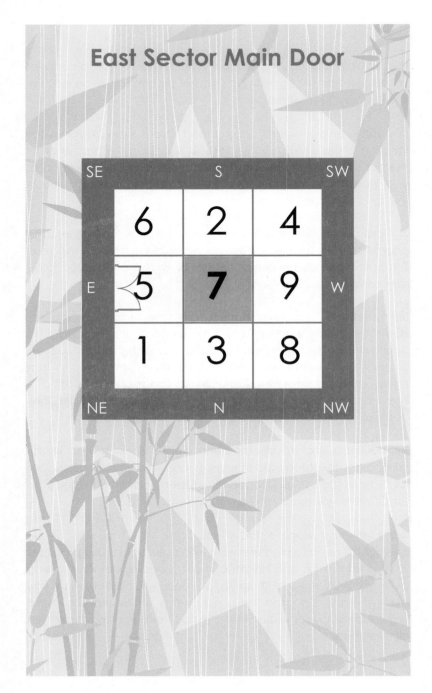

SE	S	SW
6	2	4
5 (E)	**7**	9 (W)
1	3	8
NE	N	NW

Overview

The inauspicious energy that the Five Yellow star brings is not something for you to be worried about.

In fact, you should be thankful that you know that it resides in the East sector in 2020 so that you can completely avoid it.

If your bedroom or study room happens to be in this sector, you should shift everything you have to another room. Basically, you should completely abandon and avoid this area like the plague to experience ease and comfort in all areas of your life.

Never mind about being careful in this sector. It is best to just leave it alone for the entire year because inappropriate activation of this star will lead to constant arguments, conflicts and overall, bad luck.

You wouldn't want to deal with the constant stress that this star brings, but if your Main Door happens to be in this sector, don't worry, it's not the end of the world. You can pacify its ill effects by placing metal objects made out of iron, copper, pewter or brass.

When negativity comes into your experience, that is a signal for you to turn the other way and be more positive. If you are not full of love and positivity, you will never be able to give love and positivity to others. Make it a habit to start your day with positive thoughts and feelings. Instead of reading the newspaper that is filled with negativity early in the morning, spend the wee hours focused on positive aspects that is able to nourish your mind, body, soul and spirit. The moment you open your eyes, be thankful that you are alive. Continue to meditate or pray and do something that makes your heart sing. When you are fully charged, it will be easier for you to deal with the pressure of everyday life. If you don't take care of yourself, you'll have nothing to give to others. You'll find it easier to radiate love if you are in a positive frame of mind.

Northeast Sector Main Door

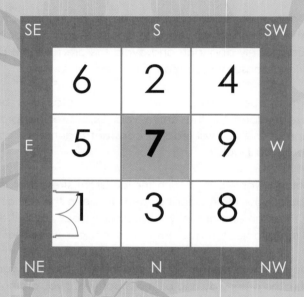

SE	S	SW
6	2	4
5 (E)	**7**	9 (W)
1	3	8
NE	N	NW

Overview

The presence of the One White star in the Northeast this year offers endless possibilities for you to receive help anytime you need it.

Having your Main Door in the direction of this Nobleman star will enable assistance to keep on coming to you in various forms. Be thankful for the benefits that you are able to tap into from this sector and notice that the more you give thanks, the more of what you are thankful for will show up in your life.

This star is also strongly linked to travel and the accumulation of wealth. But when the opportunity arises for you to go to another country, don't just travel for the sake of travelling. Although it is expected for you to take pleasure in the beauty of the place and tease your taste buds with mouth-watering delicacies, don't forget to take time to foster good relationships with new people. Participate in cultural activities and be open to meeting new friends. Basically, try to see each opportunity you come across as a chance to learn and appreciate more of life.

And when you have more money, don't forget to share your wealth with the less fortunate. Wouldn't it be better to share your money than hoarding it all to yourself? The existence of this star also serves as a reminder for you to offer a helping hand to others.

If you'd like to start a family, this is also a good sector to tap into. However, in order for this sector to help you, it needs to be supported by good landforms. A visible mountain or hill in the vicinity is a sign that you will obtain assistance from an authoritative figure.

To avoid emotional issues such as psychological complications and depression, make sure there are no water bodies or highways near your Main Door.

12-Month Room-by-Room Analysis for the Eight Types of Houses

INDEX

Using the 12-Month Outlook Based on Bedroom Location Section

To use this section, you must know the location of your property's Main Door, and the location of your bedroom. Note that your bedroom may be located on the Ground Floor or 1st or 2nd floor.

1. Identify the location of your Main Door.

In the example below, the Main Door is located in the West. So, turn to page 153 for the section on the 12-month outlook for all eight bedrooms for a West Sector Main Door.

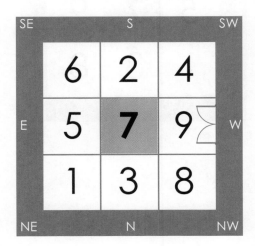

2. Identify the location of your bedroom.

In the example below, the Bedroom is located in the South. So turn to page 162, and you will find the 12-month outlook for your bedroom, located in a West Sector Main Door House.

Note: Instead of the bedroom, you can also use the same analysis for your office or study room located in that sector.

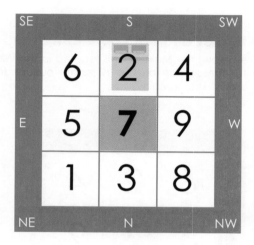

North Sector
Main Door

North Sector Main Door

This section contains the monthly outlook for all 12 months of the year for different bedroom sectors, in a property with a North Sector Main Door.

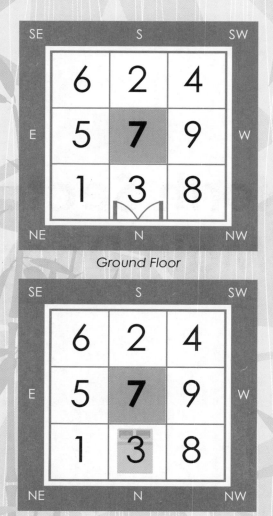

Ground Floor

First Floor

農曆正月 (February 4th - March 4th) 戊寅

This sector is beneficial for you if you are keen on making more money. However, you will most likely witness fraud or embezzlement if you are involved in business. To prevent this from happening, you should carefully monitor all business transactions and legal documents. Students who want to excel in their academic endeavours will be pleased with their achievements.

農曆二月 (March 5th - April 3rd) 己卯

Although this is not a phase in your life where you'll be as happy as a clam, it has the potential to turn into good moments if you know how to navigate through the negative situations. First of all, make sure you pay extra attention to what you're doing if you have to use heavy machinery. This will prevent any unwanted accidents from happening and if you're instincts are telling you that your colleagues have hidden agendas behind their friendly faces, you should not ignore that feeling. A bedroom placed in this sector will further aggravate the problem.

農曆三月 (April 4th - May 4th) 庚辰

It's important to remember that every thought, word and action will boomerang back into your life. In other words, what you send out will come back to you with precision. So, if you want your love life to flourish, pay attention to the energy that you are sending out to your partner. Take time to address any problem that may arise in your relationship. As far as business is concerned, pay extra attention to every detail no matter how miniscule it may seem. This will prevent unnecessary financial losses.

農曆四月 (May 5th - June 4th) 辛巳

It's best not to conclude any major deals at this time or get too excited over your accomplishments. However, if you are aware of the universal law of what you give is what you receive and the fact that everything in life is temporary, you won't be shaken by anything or anyone that tries to push you down. The grace and good karma that you have accumulated throughout your life will enable you to find the best solutions. It will attract the right people and circumstances to help you out of your problem. If you are in the counselling field, you will experience outstanding results. Using this room will enable you to continue being of service to others.

Main Door	North	Bedroom Sector	North

農曆五月 (June 5th - July 5th) 壬午

Your sphere of influence will broaden in a foreign country as you'll be given the opportunity to travel due to work related matters. While this may boost your reputation and allow you to thrive, don't ignore anything related to safety. If you have to get involved in any physically-demanding activity or sport, pay extra attention to your back area as there is potential for you to suffer from back and spine injuries.

農曆六月 (July 6th - August 6th) 癸未

Before you do or say anything to someone, imagine being in their shoes and see how you would feel if you were in their situation. While it is common for every relationship to go through problems once in a while, behaving in an irrational manner will lead to regret. There is a high chance for your relationship to flourish if you give him or her space and show more tolerance.

農曆七月 (August 7th - September 6th) 甲申

It is unwise for you to completely trust all of your friends and family members. You might be betrayed by one of them if you do that. There is also a chance for you to face a lawsuit against your own friend. The best thing for you to do to prevent further problems and emotional distress is by avoiding this sector.

農曆八月 (September 7th - October 7th) 乙酉

There is no such thing as a perfect relationship or person. It is just a matter of having the right perception. See your partner through the eyes of love. Adopt an attitude of gratitude. This will enable you to tackle any negative thoughts or feelings that tend to surface from time to time. Elderly males should be more health conscious and pay extra attention to their lungs.

農曆九月 (October 8th - November 6th) 丙戌

If you like to find excitements within gambling activities and high-risk investments, be forewarned that you will have a lesser opportunity this month in risk-taking activities. Losses are mostly caused by speculative or high-risk investments. In some extreme circumstances, it can also bode potential legal wrangles and lawsuits.

農曆十月 (November 7th - December 6th) 丁亥

Although this a good time to form alliances with partners or associates that are living in different parts of the world, it won't be smooth sailing for entrepreneurs as there is potential for employees to be involved in theft and fraud. Those who have undergone any recent surgeries should be mindful of their condition and take extra care of their health as unfortunately, there is a high chance for major complications.

農曆十一月 (December 7th 2020 - January 4th 2021) 戊子

Refrain from talking behind other people's backs. What you should do is master the art of communication and have decent face to face conversations with them. If you know how to communicate well, you will know how to rectify problems in effective ways. When it comes to money matters, there is potential for you to get involved with legal problems and financial difficulties. Therefore, it is wise for you to say no to any investment proposals related to equities, shares or any form of financial trading.

農曆十二月 (January 5th - February 2nd 2021) 己丑

The good news is, you'll be exuding with positivity and be pleased with the compatibility that you and your partner will have with each other. People will start noticing that both of you are a match made in heaven. The bad news is, there is potential for you to experience huge financial losses if you decide to dabble in gambling and speculative investments. This is a good time for you to take a prudent approach.

Main Door	North	Bedroom Sector	Northwest

農曆正月 (February 4th - March 4th) 戊寅

There is higher risk for children to get hurt by sharp metal objects. Children are also prone to get into fights at school. Parents should pay more attention and monitor their activities and behavior, respond with patience and love even when they seem particularly stubborn and sullen. This is a stage that needs to be worked out. Business plans should be put on hold, as there might be sudden changes in negotiations that could result in possible losses.

農曆二月 (March 5th - April 3rd) 己卯

If you are a property dealer or a real estate agent, you will be filling your gratitude journal with stories about how you appreciated the financial gains that came into your life because this is what you will experience, especially if there is natural water outside of this sector. While it's expected for you to be ambitious and have more connections in the real estate industry, don't forget to listen to that soft voice within that will lead you to bigger deals.

農曆三月 (April 4th - May 4th) 庚辰

Be sure to examine to see if there are any negative structures or elements outside this sector. They may indicate the possibility of lung infection for those who use the bedroom in this sector. It is best if the elderly folks, who had been afflicted with pneumonia before or suffering from weak lungs, to be temporarily moved into another room.

農曆四月 (May 5th - June 4th) 辛巳

Budding entrepreneurs, this is the time for you to prove to the world your worth! You will most likely to be off with a great start. This month, you are blessed with a favorable fortune where multiple encouraging elements will come to your assistance to help you along in your pursuits. For the salaried employees, you are most probably getting your promotion or raise that you've been eyeing.

農曆五月 (June 5th - July 5th) 壬午

Beware of any diseases that may affect your joints, muscles, and nerves. You may notice your boss is pushing for unreasonable due dates. Chances are, he or she may be worried about dropping profit margins and is taking stress and anxiety out on you. Remember not to underrate what stress could do to your wellbeing, especially when you allow the negativity affects you.

農曆六月 (July 6th - August 6th) 癸未

It's a reasonably profitable month for those concerned with agriculture, forestry or dairy business. Apart from that, this is not the time of the year to be involved in strategic negotiations, as you may end up tormented by losses in the long term. However, there'll be good profits to be made of property deals, but one might travel far to close these deals.

農曆七月 (August 7th - September 6th) 甲申

Your wealth luck may not be the best this month, and it could be that your career or business is facing some serious issues. The keyword of this month would be - Planning. Make cautious planning and consider every possible road that would maximise your profits for the year. It is essential to think thoroughly before taking any steps or make any decisions.

農曆八月 (September 7th - October 7th) 乙酉

Gastrointestinal problems will threaten those using this room. You may want to consider moving into another bedroom if you are currently using the room in this sector. Elderly folks and pregnant ladies, particularly, should avoid using this room during this time. In your workplace, beware of opponents, colleagues or even subordinates who deliberately destroy your efforts you put in at work.

農曆九月 (October 8th - November 6th) 丙戌

It will be a good month to develop even closer ties with your business partner and loved ones as your fortune is predictably fair for personal and work-life relationships. You will find your contact network crucial in building up your professional reputation and contribute to your popularity within a very short course of time.

農曆十月 (November 7th - December 6th) 丁亥

Enjoy fair health and harmonious relationship by using this sector more frequently this month especially for married couples and those committed in a relationship. You will see that it is a good time to discuss sensitive topics as both partners would be more patient and willing to hear the other one out.

農曆十一月 (December 7th 2020 - January 4th 2021) 戊子

Your personal relationship is rather bad at the beginning of the month. Be extra cautious about the malicious and insidious petty person who would trip you while you are trying to make progress in life. Think carefully before taking any actions or making any comments. However, things will be smoothened out as the month draw towards the end. It will aid you in keeping your chill and focus on phasing out dissatisfaction and arguments.

農曆十二月 (January 5th - February 2nd 2021) 己丑

You will find yourself getting some positive exposure by the media this month and this is a good time to utilise the attention in a beneficial way to further your professional and business pursuit. However, if you're in transport and travel, beware of competition and competitor. Keep your guard up as there are possible hostile takeover bids. Remain alert and try to keep ahead of your rivals. Also, the presence of negative external landforms outside this sector is most likely to cause a fire danger.

農曆正月 (February 4th - March 4th) 戊寅

You will see good development of personal relationships for those of you who use this room. Nevertheless, it will be best to make sure that no naturally-occurring water formations outside of the room. Those who wish to kick-start on a major research project, which requires quite an amount of research and development expenditure, will find this is a suitable month to scout for sponsors.

農曆二月 (March 5th - April 3rd) 己卯

If you are working or are involved in the beauty, fashion or cosmetics industry, you will easily find success and profits this month. Besides, this will be a good month to take a break from your busy schedule and go on a spiritual retreat to clear your mind. Taking some time off work will help you to regain your strength after a busy period.

農曆三月 (April 4th - May 4th) 庚辰

The positive energy in this bedroom bodes well for family and personal relationships. Couples wishing to conceive should make use of this room to make your wish come true. It's time to cash in on the real estate and property investment you had made earlier. You will be seeing a fat profit from the deals. Just be sure to control your budget to avoid extravagant spending.

農曆四月 (May 5th - June 4th) 辛巳

The reasonable utility of the media and press publicity in business will be rewarded with satisfying results. Favourable and positive attention will bring some good opportunities and operate as leverage to build a bigger client and profit base. However, couples using this bedroom may find themselves more pessimistic than usual. Be sure to be patient and communicate with each other for the benefit of the relationship.

Main Door	North	Bedroom Sector	West

農曆五月 (June 5th - July 5th) 壬午

If you know that you have been putting in good efforts and shinning your talents at the workplace, here's some good news for you! Use this room and you will be rewarded with a higher chance of getting that promotion, salary raise or recognition from your superiors this month!

農曆六月 (July 6th - August 6th) 癸未

Keep away the presence of negative structures or features outside of this sector to avoid health problems like food poisoning and/ or liver-related problems. Also, keep your temper under control, more so if you are using this sector, when you're dealing with others. Otherwise your relationship will be impacted due to your unintentionally harsh words caused by heightened anger.

農曆七月 (August 7th - September 6th) 甲申

If the academic or education field is your niche industry, you'll find this is a favourable month for you, even though your rivals threaten to sabotage your efforts. Luck is on your side thanks to your solid reputation build upon your hard work and talent. As for students due to sit for an exam soon, use this room as a study room or bedroom while preparing for your exams.

農曆八月 (September 7th - October 7th) 乙酉

Before engaging in any investment deals, it is best to seek advice from your senior or experienced professionals this month. Nothing to lose other than gaining valuable opinions that help you to make decisions. It is not the best month to indulge in the excitement of taking a random risk for momentary greed. Take the time to evaluate your decision and run it by a reliable expert, you are most likely ending up with a better reward.

農曆九月 (October 8th - November 6th) 丙戌

You might want to tap into your inner metaphysics or esoteric master in this room. The sector will allow you to understand and absorb new theories and principles better and develop your skills in the area. A sense of fulfillment will be derived from engaging completely in what you like. Furthermore, undertaking long-term investments in properties and real estate this month will be rewarded with some great earnings.

農曆十月 (November 7th - December 6th) 丁亥

Be forewarned that natural water formations outside of this room may lead to unstable and conflicting relationships. Avoid having naturally-occurring water outside of this area for prosperous and harmonious relationships. This will be a suitable month to look for sponsors if you wished to kick start on a major research project, where substantial research and development expenditure is required.

農曆十一月 (December 7th 2020 - January 4th 2021) 戊子

This is the month you will have to give it your best and work doubly hard and the fruits of hard work are just waiting to be reaped - more so if you are involved in the fashion, beauty or cosmetics business. You will see the rewards coming in double or triple depends on the amount of effort you put in. This is also a good time of the year to take a rest from your hectic schedule, go on a spiritual retreat to clear your mind and rejuvenate.

農曆十二月 (January 5th - February 2nd 2021) 己丑

If you are feeling unwell or in poor health, you are advised to avoid using this room for the entire month or else you will be prone to illness. Expectant mothers should also avoid this room as miscarriages could result. Marital stress is prevalent for couples using this room. Exercise your patience and tolerance with each other, as everyone is flawed and no one is perfect. The more efforts you put in to understand each other, the stronger your relationship will be.

| Main Door | North | Bedroom Sector | Southwest |

農曆正月 (February 4th - March 4th) 戊寅

A piece of advice for those the real estate business – adapt property-speculating method as change is needed to be able to get the most out of your investments. Keep using the same old approaches will only create undesirable scenarios. So put some effort and brainstorm to shake things up to your benefit.

農曆二月 (March 5th - April 3rd) 己卯

Watch out for the problems amongst the women, as this may bring undesirable public attention and aggression. Long-brewing issues and disagreements in the workplace could blow up disastrously if not properly solved. There will be possible serious conflicts between couples using this bedroom. Much like the previous month, a continuous effort will be needed to keep the relationship on a positive status.

農曆三月 (April 4th - May 4th) 庚辰

Pay extra attention to your kids as they could get themselves involved in rebellious or destructive activities when under the influence of the peers. Make time for your kids to get to know them more and get them to communicate with you, talk them out to stay away from bad influences. Marital relations would still be strained and tense this month. Be more tolerant and open-your-heart to hear your spouse out when dealing with them.

農曆四月 (May 5th - June 4th) 辛巳

Women may bring you troubles this month, especially if your workplace is one dominated by women. It is advisable to stay away from unnecessary arguments involving these people and focus on your work instead. Keep your head low and avoid getting into any execrable office politics.

Main Door	North	Bedroom Sector	Southwest

農曆五月 (June 5th - July 5th) 壬午

This room is extremely suitable for students and candidates due to sit for examinations soon as the energies in the sector would help in optimizing your result. The energies in this room also benefit those involved in the literary or arts field as it augurs well in looking for a company willing to publish your work. Couples will also find their relationship blossoming into something stronger and more harmonious by using this sector for the whole period of the month.

農曆六月 (July 6th - August 6th) 癸未

For the singles, should this be the most unsuitable month to start a romantic affection. So don't be too easily swept off your feet by someone you've just met at your local pub, bar or disco! For the parents, if you noticed your kids are acting more rebellious and disobedient, you may want to consider moving your kids to another room. If they continue to use this room, bear in mind that you'll have to be firmer than usual, and be prepared for some heady battle of the wills!

農曆七月 (August 7th - September 6th) 甲申

Be extra cautious when committing to important deals and avoid overlooking any hidden agendas resulting in tension. This will be especially true if the superior is female. Avoid rush into something out of spontaneous instinct. Plan carefully and take measured steps to ensure it is the right card to play.

農曆八月 (September 7th - October 7th) 乙酉

The risk of hurting yourself is relatively higher if you are using this room. So handle all sharp instruments with care. Scrutinize all legal documents very carefully before you commit yourself to them, to pre-empt any potential complications later on. Be sure to read the fine print thoroughly. Be careful about your daily interaction with people as you could be the main character of a gossip story before you realize.

農曆九月 (October 8th - November 6th) 丙戌

Success favours the most persevering, so working with the difficult clients rationally and patiently will bring you the fruit of your hard work. The energy of the month is encouraging enough for those who are required to travel for business purposes to develop their reputation and stature. So, get ready to embark on your next voyage! Long distance travel should be avoided for expectant mothers as this could result in pregnancy complications.

農曆十月 (November 7th - December 6th) 丁亥

This is not a good month to engage in speculative, high-risk investments or gambling as the fortune of wealth is certainly not in favour of this sector. Women using this room are advised to get a mammogram and body check-up on breast cancer. Even if there are no risk factors in place, it will be best to simply get yourself evaluated to ensure that all is as it should be.

農曆十一月 (December 7th 2020 - January 4th 2021) 戊子

Peach Blossom Luck is in favour for you this month! It's time to take on that vacation and you might just be lucky enough to experience an exotic romance. Keep your options open and don't cut yourself from anything just because it doesn't seem to fit into your well-organized plans. Remember to keep a low-key attitude and refrain from expecting it to develop into anything lasting. Not everything good for you need to end in forever.

農曆十二月 (January 5th - February 2nd 2021) 己丑

Threats may be found this month for those of you who are committed to relationships and marriages. Be sure not to turn small arguments into serious issues. Remember to lay low. Those who are running a business or corporate, you might find that your employees aren't very helpful this month. Avoid scheduling big projects or task that requires their high-level cooperation and input if needed. It would be a better time to work it out alone.

| Main Door | **North** | Bedroom Sector | South |

農曆正月 (February 4th - March 4th) 戊寅

Those involved in spiritual pursuits or gaining spiritual knowledge will find advantages using this bedroom. Connections to your inner spiritual master seem to be stronger this month. Employees will find that they seem to work harder but the result of income and deal closure may be unsatisfactory. It might be time to take some time off and focus your energies elsewhere.

農曆二月 (March 5th - April 3rd) 己卯

It will be a time of misunderstanding and confused thinking. Thus, relationships need to be kept in low-profile. Take some time for emotional recovery and avoid further aggravate tension between both parties. Withdraw from any arguments and suggest resolving the matter at a later time.

農曆三月 (April 4th - May 4th) 庚辰

Handle your business dealings carefully as there is high risk of being deceived and result in monetary loss. Watch your every step and keep your guard up. Avoid putting too much trust on people, especially those whom you have recently met or people new to your business concerns.

農曆四月 (May 5th - June 4th) 辛巳

Good news for those who wish to become involved in religious pursuits as this will be a good sector to advance your knowledge. At the same time, employees should make sure to resist the temptation to be drawn into arguments, gossip, and disputes in the workplace to avoid developing into large-scale issues.

North Sector Main Door

農曆五月 (June 5th - July 5th) 壬午

It will benefit you to stand up for your right this month! Do not allow anyone to storm your rights. This is not the time to sit by and watch someone else gets away with something just because they are at a higher hierarchy.

農曆六月 (July 6th - August 6th) 癸未

It is preferable not to make any big, or even life-turning decision at this point of time as confusion and lack of clarity comes into the decision-making process if you are using the bedroom. Watch out for conflicts in marriage, argument and family disharmony, and bent on to deal with any quarrels with a sense of tolerance and patience.

農曆七月 (August 7th - September 6th) 甲申

If your area of interest is within the spiritual and religious pursuits, then use this room to delve deeper into what you like. Watch out for the presence of negative structures outside of this sector as it could result in health problems such as bone-aches and joint pains. In general, while there will be money to be gained from real estate deals this month, your health may suffer. It may indicate that you could be stressed out along the way.

農曆八月 (September 7th - October 7th) 乙酉

The harmonious professional or personal relationships of yours will be threatened by misunderstandings and clouded thoughts. Maintain a low profile and allow breathing space to enable people to sort things out by themselves. At the same time, disputes and negligence may be the factor for your monetary loss, more so if you happened to be investing in property and real estate. Have your contingency plan ready as it is a month full of uncertainties.

North Sector Main Door

農曆九月 (October 8th - November 6th) 丙戌

Recognition and rewards are on their way to those with literary talents, bring along the possibility of good news and successful developments. Relationship with the in-laws for married women tends to be tense and frosty this month. You may want to consider to keep contact in a minimal especially when living under the same roof.

農曆十月 (November 7th - December 6th) 丁亥

On the professional and personal aspects of life, arguments, disputes, and backbiting are the daily undertakings, so be sure to keep your chill, as you seek solutions. Do not get involved in office politics because once you enter the game, it is harder to escape from it. Be wary of the surroundings, know what is going on but try not to get involved in matters. You might also want to check if all the fines, summonses and taxes are cleared to avoid running afoul of the law.

農曆十一月 (December 7th 2020 - January 4th 2021) 戊子

Offer some 'personal space' to your partner, if you think something is going wrong with your relationship. The best thing to do this month will be to retreat and let this cool down or blow over on its own accord. Chances are high with the windfall gains is favouring the elder female members of the families. Those of you who have previous investments might want to consider selling or cashing in as the thick earning will come to your way.

農曆十二月 (January 5th - February 2nd 2021) 己丑

Be on guard this month as rivals may pose as allies. Be skeptic, or else it would result in monetary loss. Efforts and attention shall be given to your partner. Neglecting your partner will only lead to undesirable results. For those in the literary and creative field may gain an increase in wealth with the newfound fame and enhanced reputation.

Main Door | North | Bedroom Sector | Southeast

農曆正月 (February 4th - March 4th) 戊寅

To achieve success, take advice from the coaches and mentors. If your job required strategic thinking or analysis, there will be chances to advance your career and gain a name for yourself within the corporate or industry you're in. Use this bedroom if you wish to amicably resolved a rocky relationship or business partnership.

農曆二月 (March 5th - April 3rd) 己卯

Those in positions of powers should be aware of challenges to their authority. Employers should wary of labour relations as workers might challenge the authority power and be hard to manage. There is also the possibility of indicating on the father-son relationship. Overall, relationships with substantial power differentials will face some trials and troubles this month, therefore it is essential to manage these in good faith and with an amicable resolution.

農曆三月 (April 4th - May 4th) 庚辰

This will not be very good timing to conclude and business deals as they could result in a reverse takeover, or worse case, abolish your reputation, leaving you in the losing end. Keep an eye out for disgruntled or rebellious staff, as their dissatisfaction could cause them to betray you at any given chance. Handle the problem with care and sincere interest in seeing how you can eliminate their concerns and promote a stronger sense of loyalty.

農曆四月 (May 5th - June 4th) 辛巳

The energy of this sector is ought to be favourable to the athletes and sports professionals as it would allow them to excel in competitions and tournaments this month. Children or candidates who are going to write important examinations could also tap into the energies in the room to achieve a better result. Consultants, strategists, and planners will find their skills to be in great demand.

| Main Door | North | Bedroom Sector | Southeast |

農曆五月 (June 5th - July 5th) 壬午

Look out for signs of tension for either father or son who happens to be using this bedroom. It is advisable to keep contact at a minimum level and avoid potential conflicts. The fruits of hard work come together with an equal amount of effort put in. There will be a good profit coming to your way this month but it requires a more hands-on approach to maximized rewards.

農曆六月 (July 6th - August 6th) 癸未

The energy in this bedroom is especially beneficial to couples who wished to conceive babies. It is also a favourable month for the manufacturers and those involved in the production and manufacturing industry, where output is maximized and disruptions are minimized. Elderly ladies should be mindful of any potential kidneys, organs disease, or even cancer.

農曆七月 (August 7th - September 6th) 甲申

The relationship will be in your favour this month. So it is the best time to go ahead and seal that partnership with your business partner. Remember to make sure that all terms and conditions of your agreement have been careful straighten out. If you wish to impress your superior and/or other important parties before you plan how to go about, be sure to seek advice from the mentors and elders.

農曆八月 (September 7th - October 7th) 乙酉

Refrain from involvement in speculative investment this month, but this could be a month to expand and seek new clients for the engineering business. Unexpected rewards are on their way to coming to you. Serious and immediate attention should be paid to the health issues of the elderly members in the family. Immediate medical assistance should be provided to avoid complication.

農曆九月 (October 8th - November 6th) 丙戌

Although this could be an ideal time of the year to engage yourself in property or gilt investment, always seek advice from your elders or mentors, as their suggestions will probably assist you in attaining financial success at the end of the day. Be wary of malicious parties that would sabotage your efforts.

農曆十月 (November 7th - December 6th) 丁亥

It is best to keep a low profile this month to avoid troubles and possible legal complications brought by jealousy and rivalry. It is not advisable to seek unnecessary attention unless you are ready to deal with some rather unnerving consequences. Academics and legal professionals will find their skills much desirable and will discover many opportunities opening up to further leverage their knowledge and talents.

農曆十一月 (December 7th 2020 - January 4th 2021) 戊子

Rewards will come to those who work hard as the return of their efforts, in a very short time. This is a rewarding month for prolonged effort or labour. Likewise, employees involved in the printing, logistics and courier industries can expect a promotion and salary increment this month. A general upward trend is found in those particular industries.

農曆十二月 (January 5th - February 2nd 2021) 己丑

Wealth is possible this month through opportunities and real estate. However, it doesn't come easy. Profits come only after misunderstandings and quarrels. Money is gained through attracting new clientele and customers to your business. However, you will be required to be strong and ambitious and take on your rivals headfirst to be able to attract new people. The sudden change brought upon children and young people in their work will aid and benefit them to obtain their desired results in examinations.

SE | S | SW

6	2	4
5	**7**	9
1	3	8

E | | W

NE | N | NW

農曆正月 (February 4th - March 4th) 戊寅

It is best to avoid having sharp items located in the sector of this bedroom as it may inflict stress and depression which could end up causing some form of mental instability or neurosis. This may be especially true among those who are prone to mental health issues and the elderly people using this room. Older males may find that the promotion of authority ends up in a disastrous situation.

農曆二月 (March 5th - April 3rd) 己卯

Refrain from being overambitious this month. As things will not go smoothly, you should keep a low profile on the work-front. Major decisions or career change shall be delayed, as these will not have the consequences that you intend. All minor illnesses shall be getting immediate medical attention as there is a tendency of health issues turning worse at this point.

農曆三月 (April 4th - May 4th) 庚辰

Any speculative or high-risk investments, including gambling, should be refrained from this month, as you only stand to lose more than gain. Females using this bedroom may want to go through a thorough body check and mammogram to ensure that there is no underlying health issues or risk.

農曆四月 (May 5th - June 4th) 辛巳

Always try to make effort to control your temper and frustrations by trying to reach for a solution that doesn't involve ill-will or anger, as arguments and quarrel threaten domestic harmony, more so if both are not willing to compromise. Also, watch out for heart problems or limb injuries as the energy in this bedroom contributes to increasing the risk of these health issues.

Main Door	North	Bedroom Sector	East

農曆五月 (June 5th - July 5th) 壬午

The presence of any negative structure outside of this sector shall be removed to avoid the possibility of accidents, illnesses and disastrous outcomes. Be extra cautious when making any risky business dealing and/or property transactions as fortune isn't in your favour this month. It is not wise to fully depend on your intuition when making investments. It is better not to use this room, as the risk of gastrointestinal problems is higher in this room.

農曆六月 (July 6th - August 6th) 癸未

Those involved in the publishing field are finally getting rewards and recognition for their hard work. Success and promotion may come to you, however, there is always someone in the background who will try to challenge you from an intellectual point of view. Couples using this bedroom should always keep a clear head and be careful not to allow disagreements to be blown out of proportion.

農曆七月 (August 7th - September 6th) 甲申

Those using this room should beware of niggling health issue especially in the form of eye and heart problems. Fire hazards are also a potential threat this month and electrical wiring should be examined where it is old and in need of replacement. Those in the political arena will find that friends and acquaintances will be around to lend a helping hand with their political aspirations.

農曆八月 (September 7th - October 7th) 乙酉

Conventional, long-term property deals will bring positive financial rewards, however, those in the insurance industry will need to put in more hard work to keep financial losses at bay this month. All plans of building expansion shall be delayed at this point of time. It is better to focus on consolidation and motivation for the time ahead.

農曆九月 (October 8th - November 6th) 丙戌

This month carries the risk of an upset stomach and stomach flu. It is advisable to eat more frequently at home, if not, ensure the hygiene of the food is guaranteed. Those working in the communication industry should avoid making major financial investments or making any business expansion plans this month as there are high chances of failure.

農曆十月 (November 7th - December 6th) 丁亥

Beware of the feeling of isolation and loneliness affecting your performance and daily undertakings. It is advisable to seek assistance or companion from friends and family as continuous isolation and loneliness are never good for anyone. For the candidates due to sit for examinations soon will find themselves easily distracted. Be sure to focus on your priority.

農曆十一月 (December 7th 2020 - January 4th 2021) 戊子

You should remain watchful if you are using this room, as your relationships, wealth and even safety may be in threat this month. Drive safe, make sure all necessary insurance policies are well-prepared, invest wisely, and above all, practice tolerance and patience with people around you. Indeed, it is a month to refrain from making any important decisions and investments.

農曆十二月 (January 5th - February 2nd 2021) 己丑

You will find rewards and enjoy some financial gains in speculative investments in equities and stocks, however, it is better to keep a low profile about your profits and conceal this windfall. New inspiration and ideas that lead to good financial gain will be coming to the academics and those involved in the literary field. Newly-weds are encouraged to tap into the energy of this room for enhancing growth and development.

North Sector Main Door

| Main Door | North | Bedroom Sector | Northeast |

農曆正月 (February 4th - March 4th) 戊寅

You may not be able to make much progress this month, so it's time to take a step back, reevaluate your plan and brainstorm for a new strategy for coming months. Seek advice from mentors on which path to take next. Be cautious with your interaction with the others, as you'll find romantic relationship threatened by jealousy this month.

農曆二月 (March 5th - April 3rd) 己卯

Those due to sit for important examinations will do well this month, as this room augurs well for scholarly pursuits. Speculative investment in asset purchasing will see auspicious gain this month, especially if these involve travelling abroad. It is advisable to get advice from experts if you are unsure how to proceed and, most importantly, invest wisely in these types of investments.

農曆三月 (April 4th - May 4th) 庚辰

You will see rumours being spread about you and your business, causing monetary loss and even the possibility of legal issues. Refrain from staring business partnerships or new alliances this month, as business relationships may be a little strained this month. You should be more cautious of the new connections you make; as otherwise, losses are very likely.

農曆四月 (May 5th - June 4th) 辛巳

Investment in property is very likely to see profitable deals this month. Thus, follow up on inquiries, or speak to a real estate agent to see how you can make the most out of the potential financial return and finally, make investment decisions wisely. Expectant mothers should avoid using this bedroom as there is a higher risk to encounter pregnancy complications.

Main Door	North	Bedroom Sector	Northeast

農曆五月 (June 5th - July 5th) 壬午

Fortune is in favour of those in the creative industries this month! There will be chances to make a name for yourself and step into the limelight. Take the opportunity to show your best capabilities. There is a time to step back from the limelight, and there are times when it's crucial to step forward to let your talent shine and be seen by others.

農曆六月 (July 6th - August 6th) 癸未

It's time to get that promotion you have been eyeing for! Your superior will be more than willing to recognise your talent and show their appreciation for your effort and hard work this month. However, refrain from working with people you do not know very well, as they may disappoint you when you need to rely on them the most. If you are participating in competitive sports, you will most likely do well in international competition.

農曆七月 (August 7th - September 6th) 甲申

Fortune is in your favour this month! Your can easily conclude any business deals as everything will go smooth. Those in travel and logistics industries will be able to close new deals and build partnerships abroad. Those in the real estate industry will find highly lucrative deals at this point of time. Many good offers are in the property market, don't forget to check out some good bargain as well.

農曆八月 (September 7th - October 7th) 乙酉

Relationships will be tense this month in both your personal life and the workplace. It will not be a good idea to focus on romance, as it may leave you disappointed, or even worse, your reputation tarnished. The workplace is extra competitive this month, as office politics is at its full height. In spite of this, those in the financial industry are likely to find new clients and customers.

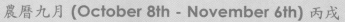

農曆九月 (October 8th - November 6th) 丙戌

The room will bring benefits to those due to sit for important examinations this month. The energies in the room is conducive for learning and academic activities, assisting you to concentrate and tackle problems with a clear mind. Politicians looking to improve their status will receive support from people with high authority within the government, or within their respective parties.

農曆十月 (November 7th - December 6th) 丁亥

As projects tend to stagnate and progress is halted, it is advisable to reexamine your position this month. Take a step back, conserve your energy and plan for a later stage. Those who are in a committed relationship should be careful not to let jealousy ruin your romantic relationship.

農曆十一月 (December 7th 2020 - January 4th 2021) 戊子

Outstation speculative investments in asset acquisition will see favourable profits this month, so take the chance to travel as there will be possible financial rewards. Energies in this bedroom augur well for scholarly pursuit, so those sitting for important examinations should tap into the energies of the room for a better academic outcome.

農曆十二月 (January 5th - February 2nd 2021) 己丑

If you're single and on the lookout, then this is the month when romance could happen for you! Make an effort to expand your social circle and meet new people. Those who are in the logistics industry may go through a challenging month. At the same time, it may not be the best month to hire new people, as it could result in getting unsuitable employees who would cause you more loss than gain.

East Sector
Main Door

Main Door	East	Bedroom Sector	East

This section contains the monthly outlook for all 12 months of the year for different bedroom sectors in a property with an East Main Door.

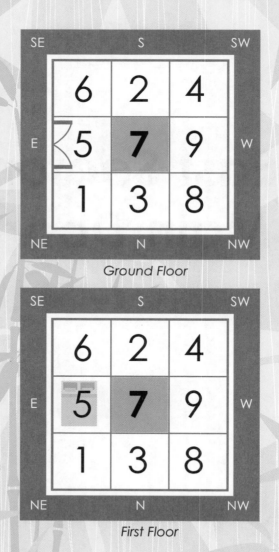

Ground Floor

First Floor

農曆正月 (February 4th - March 4th) 戊寅

This would be an overwhelming month for some, as stress and pressure from work will affect relationships. Take time to talk things out, clear any misunderstandings that you may have, so that your partner understands your situation. Your stress is probably caused by betrayal in the workplace. If that is the case, stay strong and focus on what you can do. Avoid involvement in office politics as much as possible.

農曆二月 (March 5th - April 3rd) 己卯

Refrain from involvement in high-risk property deals as the outcome could be unfavourable. Be extremely cautious and take conservative approach in your financial activities. Professional and personal relationships tend to be quite tense. It is advisable to walk away from any possible arguments or conflicts before things turn worse.

農曆三月 (April 4th - May 4th) 庚辰

If traveling is in your planned schedule this month, then it is best to make sure all the necessary insurance policies are in place. Do not trust your belongings with someone new, even if they seem friendly and genuine. Travel safe and be particularly careful and alert. Keep your valuables and important documents close at all times.

農曆四月 (May 5th - June 4th) 辛巳

Those using this bedroom should beware of any signs of mental issues. Such condition requires immediate treatment as it could lead to severe complications if left untreated. One should not feel ashamed when it comes to seeking early psychiatric assistance or counseling. Head injuries and bones problems are also prevalent this month, so be extra cautious and avoid partaking any risky and dangerous physical activities.

East Sector Main Door

農曆五月 (June 5th - July 5th) 壬午

Singles should avoid diving head-first into any new relationship this month, as this will probably result in heartbreaks. If you choose to enter a new relationship nonetheless, keep a lighthearted approach and try to enjoy the moments as they last. Females who have been suffering from stomach upset and abdominal pain lately should consult the doctor soonest. This could be sign to something more serious.

農曆六月 (July 6th - August 6th) 癸未

Refrain from being overambitious - stick to a practical plan and be wise when doing property transactions. Couples who find their relationship going through a bumpy road this month should give each other some space to calm down and think things over. It will only bring undesirable consequences if issues are pressed to breaking point. Those who have been bothered by illnesses lately, especially stomach problems, should seek immediate medical treatment.

農曆七月 (August 7th - September 6th) 甲申

Be forewarned that relationships may face some setbacks this month. Those using this room should prepare yourself for issues that may crop up. There could be involvement of a third party. However, all is not doom and gloom; there will be plenty of opportunities for improvement if both parties remain honesty and open-minded. Be careful in choosing your words when communicating with each other.

農曆八月 (September 7th - October 7th) 乙酉

Women using this room may be prone to respiratory and digestion problems this month. Athletes and those who play sports competitively should be wary of accidents which could cause bone and tendon injuries. Do not ignore any warning signs of injuries and leave them untreated as these could cause complications in the future.

農曆九月 (October 8th - November 6th) 丙戌

It would be a rather difficult month for legal professionals to put their points across and argue their case successfully. It's best to delay any legal issue that involves litigation for the meantime, or settle these as soon as possible, as your chances of winning the case in court are slim. Bear in mind to be patient in addressing any misunderstandings and disagreements with family members and loved ones.

農曆十月 (November 7th - December 6th) 丁亥

Watch out for any negative structures or features facing this room as these could trigger emotional or mental problems such as stress and depression for those using this room. Other than being prone to anxiety and stress, other types of health may also arise in the form of headaches or migraines. Take care of your well-being and be mindful not to let stress at work take a toll on your mental and emotional health.

農曆十一月 (December 7th 2020 - January 4th 2021) 戊子

Some personal setbacks are expected this month, especially for those in the entertainment industry. Remain focused on your business goal while taking care of your personal affairs at the same time. Decisions for joint-venture or partnership may be delayed. It's best to wait for a more suitable time to put the plans into action. Refrain from rushing into something even if your intuition tells you it is the right thing to do, as intuitions may be clouded by other factors as well.

農曆十二月 (January 5th - February 2nd 2021) 己丑

Good fortune is in store for those due to sit for a major examination. You're likely to get desirable results this month! Successful outcomes will also await those required to travel for work and business purposes. Couples will find that relationship is more harmonious and that your partner is as equally committed as you are this month.

East Sector Main Door

農曆正月 (February 4th - March 4th) 戊寅

Those in the property business will find this month especially difficult in terms of achieving mental clarity, as it is hard to resolve problems completely from the cause. You'll feel like your ability to make decisions is clouded this month. In such situation, it is advisable to defer your decision to a later time when your mind is refreshed and clearer. Elderly males using this room should beware of potential head injuries or head-related symptoms and illness.

農曆二月 (March 5th - April 3rd) 己卯

This will not be the best month to carry out offshore and negotiations, as concluding them now could lead to potential loss. It might be best to delay the plans for a more favourable time in the future. The presence of negative structures outside of this room could affect the academic performance of those due to sit for examinations. You might want to consider moving into another for the duration of the examinations.

農曆三月 (April 4th - May 4th) 庚辰

Brace yourself for a rocky journey this month as luck hasn't been in your favour. Betrayals occur and people turn against you, spreading rumours about your business may lead to legal problems. At the same time, your business relationship will also be affected and turn tense. You should always be prepared to work out solutions to avoid reputation being tarnished by those rumours. In such situation where you will be under a heavy load of stress, take the space and solitary time you need and ensure you get adequate amounts of rest.

農曆四月 (May 5th - June 4th) 辛巳

Elderly males should prioritize their health this month. Visit your doctor even if it seems to be a minor problem. Early treatments are always better than medical complications at a later stage. You will find good real estate deals, however, you will need to be very careful in choosing the correct one to avoid unnecessary loss.

East Sector Main Door

農曆五月 **(June 5th - July 5th)** 壬午

Avoid making any major financial decisions this month as the risk of being deceived is higher. Delay any decisions involving a big amount of money to a later time. Romance doesn't seem to go well as well, as relationships come under tension as one or both parties may be tempted into illicit affairs, and in some cases, leads to marital break-ups and separation.

農曆六月 **(July 6th - August 6th)** 癸未

Contracts and agreements should be carefully checked to ensure everything is in order before dropping your signature, especially those in the entertainment industry who intended to expand their business. It may cost you a fortune for oversights and mistakes. Relationships are likely to be short-term so do not invest a high hope for it to be forever. Not saying that you should avoid socializing and pleasant flirtations, just keep things in perspective to avoid disappointment or getting hurt.

農曆七月 **(August 7th - September 6th)** 甲申

Real estate and property business are highly profitable this month, just be sure to grab that opportunity as they come up. Taking some calculated risk could yield big dividends and benefits. Remember to care for your spouse too when you're busy making money, after all, he/she is one of the reasons why you are working so hard.

農曆八月 **(September 7th - October 7th)** 乙酉

Relationship disharmonious is possible this month, as there will be jealousy that occurred. Beware of the green-eyed monster jeopardizing your relationship using pent-up resentments. Be ready to talk openly when discussing the issues at the root of insecurity of your spouse or partner. Remain a sincere attitude in the discussion and walk in your partner's or spouse's shoes to understand them better.

農曆九月 (October 8th - November 6th) 丙戌

Watchful on what you say and do as personal reputations could be called into question this month. Impulsive words and behavior could bring serious consequences. Understand that all your actions will be under observation, so don't make offensive statements or jokes unless you're ready to defend your point-of-view to those who are keen to make you so do.

農曆十月 (November 7th - December 6th) 丁亥

This is a rather difficult month for those in the property industry, as judgments and decisions are often hazed. It is best to delay any major decision-making. If important decisions need to be made, seek suggestions and advice from those who can view the picture clearly without any potential confusion. Elderly males should be cautious about head injuries this month.

農曆十一月 (December 7th 2020 - January 4th 2021) 戊子

Refrain from having negative structures outside of this room, as it is likely to affect the academic performance of children. Take the necessary steps to ensure that their concentrate and focus are not disturbed. You might want to consider moving them into another room to help them achieve the mental peace needed for their studies benefits.

農曆十二月 (January 5th - February 2nd 2021) 己丑

This is a month to tap into the energy of the room is you wish to develop your spiritual cultivation. You are likely to achieve your desirable result with half the effort. On the other hand, the fortune in relationships seems to be out of the picture. Beware falling into disputes and arguments at the workplace for those working as salaried employees, as it might lead to legal issues if arguments get nasty or serious. In alike conditions, romantic relationships will also found embroiled in quarrels and arguments.

| Main Door | East | Bedroom Sector | North |

農曆正月 (February 4th - March 4th) 戊寅

Be watchful on your personal belongings and your material assets, there is a likelihood of wealth loss caused by fraud or theft. Valuable jewellery should be kept in a safe and hidden place. Remember to be attentive to your personal documents – especially those relating to your financial account and statements. It is advisable to keep confidential business documents in a well-guarded location.

農曆二月 (March 5th - April 3rd) 己卯

Parents should avoid placing the male teenagers in this room, as they may turn out to be more rebellious than usual. Consider tempering their spirit and soften their hard edges by changing room. If so happens your child is going through his rebellious stage, refrain from engaging in pointless battle of wills. Be understanding and give necessary space to earn their independence. This will work much better in the long run for both parties.

農曆三月 (April 4th - May 4th) 庚辰

This will be a favourable month for those in the real estate or property development business, as revenue comes together with the amount of effort put in. Visualize and focus the future as you make plans for the present. Similarly, service industry specialists will find this month to be a rewarding month for their business. Just make sure that all taxes due are paid off or else the long arm of the law may soon catch up with you.

農曆四月 (May 5th - June 4th) 辛巳

Be prepared that a stormy relationship will be reaching its end at some point of this month, regardless of personal or professional. Think in a way that it's better to sever bad ties now, instead of allowing them to bog you down. Be sure not to let emotions get the better of you, remain clear-eyed and be practical, to avoid making poor decisions.

Main Door	East	Bedroom Sector	North

農曆五月 (June 5th - July 5th) 壬午

Threats from your rivals and competitors to you and your business interest may arrive unexpectedly, with a purpose to takeover of your enterprise. Be prepared to take necessary steps to defend your business. Be forewarned that this is not the best timing to scout for deals, as even those that are already in the midst of being negotiated may take time to conclude. Financial losses are likely this month but an important lesson can be learned through the process.

農曆六月 (July 6th - August 6th) 癸未

This is a good month to close property deals but, be extra cautious on the details as it could cost you a fortune, or even worse, lead to legal issues if one is not careful enough. Let your inner nitpicker run wild in this situation! On the contrary, your relationships are going downhill this month, so do not make important decisions. It will be best to let things slide for the time being and don't forget to take some time to properly address discords in your marital relationship.

農曆七月 (August 7th - September 6th) 甲申

Avoid using this room if you've been feeling rather under the weather, as the energies in the room could well leverage your situation or any internal injuries from which you're already suffering. At the same time, beware of fraud or theft and ensure that all official papers to oversee your finances are in place. It is advisable not to trust people too quickly, especially the newcomers in your life.

農曆八月 (September 7th - October 7th) 乙酉

Energies in this room will favour those who required to travel in some form this month. Clarity of thought is coming to assistance to those who need to make major decisions this month, so take this opportunity to think things through and decide now instead of postponing decision-making to another time. Do not believe in unusual good investment deals as this may cause unnecessary monetary loss and legal troubles.

農曆九月 (October 8th - November 6th) 丙戌

You will need to monitor your employees closely, as even formerly loyal staff may attempt to deceive or steal from you if you let your guard down. All necessary precautionary measures should be duly enforced and executed. At the same time, important decision-making about your business deals should be postponed to risking slander and other types of disputes unnecessarily.

農曆十月 (November 7th - December 6th) 丁亥

Be attentive to your state of mind, as emotional stress and fatigue could lead to mild depression. Spend more time with friends who make you see the bright side of things if you need to, to avoid focusing too much on the negativity. Pay extra attention to details of business deals and contracts, especially the fine print, to minimize the risk of being deceived.

農曆十一月 (December 7th 2020 - January 4th 2021) 戊子

If you noticed any negatives forms outside this room, you should mind for your safety, as the tragedy of being robbed or mugged is possible this month. Refrain from involving in any family dispute or arguments, as there is a likelihood that the situation will develop into serious issues.

農曆十二月 (January 5th - February 2nd 2021) 己丑

Be attentive to the ailments affecting your abdominal area, stomach or pancreases. You will need to tread carefully this month, as hidden agendas may leave negative effects on your business. Before concluding any deals, be sure that you have fully understood what you're in for, particularly on the small details. On the domestic front, especially between mother and daughter-in-law, possible troubles have arisen from misunderstandings. Be fair and tactful in handling such scenarios, or you might risk worsening the situation.

Main Door	East	Bedroom Sector	Northwest

農曆正月 (February 4th - March 4th) 戊寅

You will be obtaining an unexpected force to assist you in reviving stagnant career and business this month. You will find ventures getting a fresher start, but you must be ready to think and work slightly differently. Focusing on academic activities and educational improvement is beneficial to the adults, as the outcome is good these endeavours, resulting in a stronger interest in self-cultivation.

農曆二月 (March 5th - April 3rd) 己卯

Good news to property and real estate investors! You will find bumper financial profit making its way to you this month. Your relationship will see a positive and harmonious outcome this month, and obstructions will melt away before you even realise. It is ideal for you to capitalize and make use of those relationships to bring yourself a greater professional opportunity in the future.

農曆三月 (April 4th - May 4th) 庚辰

Extra earnings are possible this month. Check your list of portfolios and execute plans that in line with marketing trends. Do not hesitate to utilize your contact network and bring in more new clients, as this is an ideal time to nurture new business relationships or partnerships.

農曆四月 (May 5th - June 4th) 辛巳

Well-planned ambitious projects shall be embarked this month, as fortune is in the house for you. You're likely to enjoy support from your superior, so take the chance to consult them for valuable advice and insider tricks that could assist to achieve your desired outcome. Investors involved in the property and real estate business will find this month to be a fairly profitable one, as will traders involved in the futures, stock and equities market.

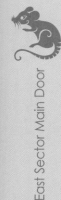

| Main Door | East | Bedroom Sector | Northwest |

農曆五月 (June 5th - July 5th) 壬午

This month is not favourable for risk-taking decisions, especially in finances and relationships. It is better to deposit your money in the bank instead of using it to engage in speculative property investments. Relationship-wise, it is advisable to give the other party some space of his/her own and wait for a more appropriate time to act.

農曆六月 (July 6th - August 6th) 癸未

It will be the best time to make use of your network of contact for those in the management, marketing or consultancy line, and be proactive in looking for new possibilities to expand your business to previously unexplored markets. Profits are possible from all deals concluded abroad, as long as legal documents are perused thoroughly before signing it.

農曆七月 (August 7th - September 6th) 甲申

Good progress is in favour this month, regardless of personal or workplace. Couples using this room will see a harmonious relationship growing strong. You will also see desirable progress in the workplace, resulting in employees being recognized for their effort and be rewarded accordingly. This creates a general sense of well-being in the workplace causes increased productivity from you and achieving targets at a better pace than expected.

農曆八月 (September 7th - October 7th) 乙酉

Keep a sharp eye open for opponents, subordinates or colleagues who grit to sabotage your efforts. Being kind and trusting are both noble qualities but sometimes a steel-heart and an intimidating front can be of use in warding off the insincere people around. Despite the petty persons, you will enjoy harmony and bliss in your relationships this month. So make the most of the positive vibes and strengthen the bonds between you and your loved ones, and business partners within this favourable period.

農曆九月 (October 8th - November 6th) 丙戌

The energies of the month augur well for short-term gains from speculative investments, however, always be extra cautious and remain a modest attitude with money activities. Health-wise, be attentive to bladder or kidney problems and seek immediate medical attention if any signs of unwell show up. Remember not to overwork and overexert yourself. You will have to learn to manage stress level wisely and know that no matter how successful you may be, there will always be jealous parties out there trying to take you down. Just make sure that you are honest to yourself.

農曆十月 (November 7th - December 6th) 丁亥

Couples using this room will have the wind in your sail and enjoy harmonious relationships this month. Indeed, this is a good time to start a new venture or project, with possible positive outcomes. You will find obstacles melting away in the face of any issues, so don't hesitate to embark on the ambitious projects you've long put on hold.

農曆十一月 (December 7th 2020 - January 4th 2021) 戊子

Be mindful of jealousy co-workers who carry malevolence. It is best to keep a low-profile in the workplace, but at the same time, understand that you can't get everyone to like you. Be wary not to reveal any important information during discussions and leisure chatting, otherwise leaked information will be used against you in an unexpected situation. Your relationship with your spouse will flourish and remain harmonious after a slightly rocky start to the month, as long as both parties are frank to each other.

農曆十二月 (January 5th - February 2nd 2021) 己丑

Fortune of wealth this month is favourable to those who work closely with their network of contact and business partners to secure revenue. However, bear in mind that the key to success and well-balanced life is always moderation. Avoid overworking or neglecting your health, as you will be prone to fatigue, stress, cardiac problems, and eye ailments. Fire hazard is possible this month, hence be sure to get a qualified electrician to check on the wiring and electrical system of your home and workplace to avoid tragedy.

Main Door	East	Bedroom Sector	West

SE   S   SW

6	2	4
5	**7**	9
1	3	8

E   W

NE   N   NW

East Sector Main Door

農曆正月 (February 4th - March 4th) 戊寅

Students should tap into the energies in this room, as it is beneficial to education, learning, and scholarly activities. Meanwhile, your personal and professional relationship will be smooth-sailing this month, so it's time to cultivate closer ties with your loved ones and your business partners.

農曆二月 (March 5th - April 3rd) 己卯

Money is possible for those willing to work hard and take calculated risks in the cosmetics and fashion industries. Take the opportunity to promote your products to as many markets as possible. The positive energies in this room should also be harness by those in the political field to gain support at the grassroots.

農曆三月 (April 4th - May 4th) 庚辰

A harmonious relationship is coming to your way for couples or those in a relationship. Make use of this month for some heart-to-heart conversations about issues and potential issues that may occur. The smooth energy enables you to push aside arguments and discover solutions or a compromise that benefits both of you. Indeed, this is the perfect time to pop that question to your loved one!

農曆四月 (May 5th - June 4th) 辛巳

Refrain having any negative structures or features outside this room to avoid potential fire hazards. For business owners, rivals and competitors shall be keep-an-eye on as risk of a hostile takeover may occur this month. It is advisable to remain vigilant for any underhand or aggressive tactics to bring about their downfall.

| Main Door | East | Bedroom Sector | West |

農曆五月 (June 5th - July 5th) 壬午

It is not a month to indulge in risk-taking activities, especially those engaging in metal, futures, equities or stock trading. Avoid rushing into anything recklessly simply because you want to make a quick kill. It is best to remain disciplined and careful this month. Challenging or questioning your superior wouldn't be the wisest move, as your attempts are most likely to end in defeat and embarrassment.

農曆六月 (July 6th - August 6th) 癸未

It's a month to be extra attentive to your health issues. Seek advice from the doctors at the first sign of trouble, to ensure you get early treatments for diseases such as eye or heart disease, or even leukaemia. As your thoughts may be clouded this month, you should avoid making major decisions. It is best to exercise tolerance and endurance this month unless you wish to land into hot soup. Be sure to think thoroughly before you act.

農曆七月 (August 7th - September 6th) 甲申

The energy in this room will not be in favour of the students, scholars, and candidates due to sit for examinations this month. Consider moving into another room for a clearer mind and sharper focus ability would be a wise move. Female employees may find it hard to gain support from their superiors, so watch your back and take every step carefully, seek for necessary approval in black-and-white before you undertake any important decisions.

農曆八月 (September 7th - October 7th) 乙酉

You will find this month rewarding in terms of recognition and praise, especially if you had been working very hard and portrait high productivity in the past few months. Those in the counseling, advisory and psychology fields will also find their advice and skills much sought-after.

農曆九月 (October 8th - November 6th) 丙戌

This month, good romance luck will come to those using this room. Those of you already in a relationship, you will see the wind in your sail and enjoy a relatively trouble-free month; while the singles will meet new people who will prove to be interesting romantic potential. However, patience and thorough consideration are needed in handling tacky situations, as acting hastily will only bring undesirable consequences.

農曆十月 (November 7th - December 6th) 丁亥

Take this opportunity to cultivate closer ties with your business partners and loved ones, as this will be a great month of making great strides in both professional and personal relationships. So be sure to make the most out of this month and boost relationships with colleagues and superiors.

農曆十一月 (December 7th 2020 - January 4th 2021) 戊子

Pursuits of the spiritual and religious should tap into the energy of this room. It will enable you to meditate and develop mind-power, help you focus on your mind and power, and will spill over into the other aspects of your life. Likewise, politician or budding ones who harness the positive energies of the month are most likely to take on their opponent at the grassroots level.

農曆十二月 (January 5th - February 2nd 2021) 己丑

You will see a good financial gain for those offload property from the property portfolio. Always remember to think twice and think thoroughly before acting. It is best for expectant mothers to stay away from this room. Otherwise, you risk some complications or even a possible miscarriage. Any remarks or information at face value shall be reevaluated, as you are surrounded by people who are only out to look after their own interest.

農曆正月 (February 4th - March 4th) 戊寅

This is a good month to enter that property deal you had been eyeing for, so be ready to make the right move when opportunity strikes! Elderly women using this room may face problems of strokes and migraines; it will be wise to be attentive to any of the warning signs as early as possible. Do not ignore any signs of illness to avoid complications.

農曆二月 (March 5th - April 3rd) 己卯

It is better to stay away from quarrels and disputes this month as they may lead to violent consequences. This is especially true if you find your temper fraying easily and quite frequently. Instead of saying what's on your mind, it is best to heed the sage advice of not saying anything at all if one can't be compelled to say anything nice!

農曆三月 (April 4th - May 4th) 庚辰

Those using this room will find unfriendly competition, or even intense rivalry this month. The negative energies in this room will also bring about emotional and psychological issues for those who unintentionally tap into them, so it will be best to be on guard against explosive arguments in both professional and personal relationships.

農曆四月 (May 5th - June 4th) 辛巳

You will find marital relationship tenser this month. It would be better to give each other space. Indeed, it would be wiser to keep your contact with your in-laws to a minimal, to save yourself and your partner off of unnecessary stress. Try not to get in each other's way and it could a long way towards easing the tension.

Main Door	East	Bedroom Sector	Southwest

農曆五月 (June 5th - July 5th) 壬午

This could a favourable month for the writers, as the time has come to look for a publisher who's willing to publish your work. Make use of the beneficial time and make a name for yourself from it! Those involved in extensive research and development will find positive outcomes and financial benefits bring about from changes within the organization.

農曆六月 (July 6th - August 6th) 癸未

Investment in high-risk, speculative deals is likely to obtain favourable return this month, as all negotiations will have the likelihood of going well. At the same time, it is the ideal time of the year to expand your social circle and meet new people, and see whether your efforts will land you a romantic encounter or otherwise! Beware of some sudden changes or last-minute issues for those travelling this month, which necessitate the buying of travel insurance.

農曆七月 (August 7th - September 6th) 甲申

Workplace satisfaction is one of the important element to ensure your company achieve the desired result. You will find that fair-paid and well-recognized employees are more loyal and loyalty workers are likely to go the extra mile in achieving the result you desire. You might want to, however, scrutinize all legal documents before signing them, to avoid the possibility of any legal complication later on.

農曆八月 (September 7th - October 7th) 乙酉

This a good month to engage in business expansion or build partnerships abroad. However, you must scrutinize all legal documents and read the fine print before dropping your signature to the dotted line. Most importantly, you need to be certain of your obligations as far as any legally binding contract is concerned. It would also be wise to stay away from disputes and quarrels, as things may take a turn for the worse.

農曆九月 (October 8th - November 6th) 丙戌

If you wish your professional and personal relationships to remain harmonious and long-termed, then this is a favourable month to foster even closer ties with your business partners, co-workers, and loved ones. Women in the entertainment industry will see this a rewarding month, in terms of recognition and promotion. Stature and reputation will also be greatly enhanced for those who find it necessary to travel in the name of business.

農曆十月 (November 7th - December 6th) 丁亥

Watch out for potential health issues involving the liver for those using this room. Females should also go through a thorough check-up to eliminate any risk of cancer. As for business owners and entrepreneurs, be sure that all your deals are above-board or you risk facing the full brunt of the law. Playing with fire in the legal sense this month could certainly backfire in a bad way, so it will be best to err on the side of caution.

農曆十一月 (December 7th 2020 - January 4th 2021) 戊子

Pregnant women should avoid using this room this month, to prevent any pregnancy complications or a miscarriage. Keep any potential risks at bay by moving into another room for the time being. However, those preparing for examinations can be optimistic in the hope of positive outcomes in their papers.

農曆十二月 (January 5th - February 2nd 2021) 己丑

Kidney and blood circulatory system complications should be paid attention to for those using this room this month. The atmosphere is pretty tense between you and your partner, as relationship is affected due to possible interference by a third party. If you're working in the tourism, courier and logistics field, you'll find yourself having to double your efforts this month. Help and support will not be forthcoming, but don't give up just yet, as perseverance will eventually pay off.

| Main Door | East | Bedroom Sector | South |

農曆正月 (February 4th - March 4th) 戊寅

This room is best suit for those in religious pursuits or for gaining spiritual knowledge. You will find enlightenment come easier than usual. However, this room could make use of your mental and emotional stress and turn it into depression or hallucinations when accumulated to a certain level. It will be important for you to talk to people close to you or seek professional help if you find yourself increasingly disoriented and confused, and unable to cope with regular, day-to-day problems that you had no problem with before.

農曆二月 (March 5th - April 3rd) 己卯

This could be a rather difficult month for those in merchant banking, shares, stocks, and equities as deals go belly up in many cases and profits start to decrease. You will need to think fast and find ways to stop potential disasters and catastrophes. Do not hesitate to seek advice from others and discuss strategies to see how you can play the game a little different.

農曆三月 (April 4th - May 4th) 庚辰

Usage of this room this month could increase the occurrence of argument, which results in disharmony and could threaten the tranquility of home-life. So where possible, avoid using this bedroom. All monetary deals should be carefully evaluated, as otherwise, you could well end up being duped by unscrupulous parties. Be extra cautious to all that takes place verbal negotiation and meticulously read through the fine print in contracts and documents.

農曆四月 (May 5th - June 4th) 辛巳

In the workplace, you may find your employees more hard-headed than usual, thereby compromising their ability to think and plan logically. This could lead to bad decision-making and causes financial losses to your company. Take good care of your eyes, any ailments or problems affecting them will only cause your health, and peace of mind, to suffer this month.

農曆五月 (June 5th - July 5th) 壬午

This is not the month to take risk with your health. It is best to seek immediate medical attention if any sign of unwell shows its traits, to prevent nagging or recurring ailments. Those who ventured interest in spiritual and religion subjects should harness the energies of the room, as it could well produce spiritual or religiously-inclined persons.

農曆六月 (July 6th - August 6th) 癸未

Refrain from signing any documents or contract this month as they may not be what they seem. Be sure to read the fine prints, and pay attention to what's being said in between the lines. Arguments and family disharmony could occur for those using this room as well, so think before you speak. Students may want to consider moving into another room as the negative energies in this room could have bad effects on academic performance.

農曆七月 (August 7th - September 6th) 甲申

Wealth should be at the top of your concern this month. Be careful with that new property deals that seem too good to be true, spend some extra bit of time to verify credentials to avoid financial losses. Avoid participating in negative socializing activities, such as gambling, and avoid temptations that require use of substance, or some form of risk-taking with money.

農曆八月 (September 7th - October 7th) 乙酉

The real estate is making money on property deals this month, so it's time to take that step to change your home. The market is good for properties at this point, and you could make some favourable profits. Just make sure that all the legal issues are well taken care of. Be sure to read documents and fine prints carefully or consult a lawyer when in doubt so that possible losses can be avoided.

農曆九月 (October 8th - November 6th) 丙戌

Conflicts and disharmony are expected between the in-laws. It's time to practice tolerance and endurance with them and deal with problems as it arises. Be wary of your spleen and other internal organs, unless you wish to acquire ailments affecting them, which could lead to more serious health problems in the long run. Money is possible this month from your investments in properties using your experience, knowledge, and expertise in the real estate field.

農曆十月 (November 7th - December 6th) 丁亥

Where possible, this room should be avoided by couples, as the energies presented will not augur well for their relationship. At the same time, it is best to avoid significant investments or embark on new projects this month. You are most likely going to experience loses from poor decision-making from cloudy thoughts and weak reasoning this month.

農曆十一月 (December 7th 2020 - January 4th 2021) 戊子

The energies of the room will bring benefits to medical professionals and practitioners this month. You will find a boost to your reputation and the increasing number of patients who will prefer your service. However, pregnant women should avoid using this room, and seek advice from the doctor, to prevent the occurrence of miscarriage or any form of pregnancy complications.

農曆十二月 (January 5th - February 2nd 2021) 己丑

Students and scholars sitting for important examinations this month should use this room as the energies in it bodes well for studies and revision. Those working in the media and marketing industries will find this month full of achievements and honour, so get ready to enjoy your moment in the spotlight! Your past effort and labours will finally get its recognition. However, people using this room might have to fight some emotional volatility and psychological issues, so take extra care if you're already prone to depression and mental instability.

Main Door	East	Bedroom Sector	Southeast

農曆正月 (February 4th - March 4th) 戊寅

If you are working in the research and development field, you will most likely find opportunities to advance your career and make a name for yourself in the industry – so don't be hesitant in putting your best foot forward and making strategic attempts to improve your reputation. Extra money is possible for those in the logistics, courier and tourism business this month.

農曆二月 (March 5th - April 3rd) 己卯

The energies in the room benefit long-term investment activities. The likelihood to see the return of profit is high this month. However, refrain from making any short-term investments. Those in positions of power should be aware of challenges to their authority. You may have to deal with rebellious subordinates or colleagues who are bent on undermining your authority.

農曆三月 (April 4th - May 4th) 庚辰

You may find business endeavours appear to be more challenging than usual. It's time to consult an expert or someone wiser to improve your luck this month. Be sure to be humble and get different opinions from as many people as you can. These could prove to be eye-opening and useful in more ways than one.

農曆四月 (May 5th - June 4th) 辛巳

There will be a substantial financial gain to be made from speculative investment and stocks, however, it is only wise not to flaunt your wealth. This could be a rather favourable month for those involved in the consultancy or any other field that requires strategic thinking, as your reputation will be greatly enhanced through the good work that you produced.

| Main Door | East | Bedroom Sector | Southeast |

農曆五月 (June 5th - July 5th) 壬午

Employees and workers in the engineering industry will likely receive support from their superiors. However, in general, this is the time to maintain a low profile, and focus on your core competency. Any important decisions such as expanding your business should be postponed to the right time. Refrain from all forms of investment, especially the high-risk ones, to minimise the risk of any consequential legal problems.

農曆六月 (July 6th - August 6th) 癸未

Family relations are strained and tense this month. It is best to wait for a better time to have heart-to-heart conversations. This is a month of potential scams and betrayal, which could cause financial setbacks or even legal complications. Likewise, it is not advisable to conclude business deals this month to avoid potential reverse takeovers.

農曆七月 (August 7th - September 6th) 甲申

Couples will enjoy a harmonious and blissful month in terms of relationship. Those in speculative investment or stock and equities industry are most likely to see good profit heading your way. This is also a good month to travel for both business and leisure, especially for those involved in research and development ventures.

農曆八月 (September 7th - October 7th) 乙酉

Employers and bosses may find their authority and decision being challenged by rebellious staff this month. Be patient and seek to understand your employee's points of view to achieve mutual understanding. Minor health issues are in sight this month. Do not ignore these as it could lead to more serious conditions, and may require greater medical treatment and care further down the road, so it is best to get them sorted out early.

農曆九月 **(October 8th - November 6th)** 丙戌

This month, luck is on your side! You will see notable financial gains from investment, especially in real estate and property. You will also enjoy a harmonious relationship with your partner. Therefore, be sure to take this opportunity to foster even closer ties with your loved ones.

農曆十月 **(November 7th - December 6th)** 丁亥

Beware of rivals and competitors who are bent on bringing you down. This applies for both business owners and salaried employees trying to make a decent living. It would be best to focus on what you are doing and maintain a low profile to minimise the possibility of running into trouble. At the same time, you may also want to stay away from office politics.

農曆十一月 **(December 7th 2020 - January 4th 2021)** 戊子

Health issues may need to be at the top of your concern list this month for those using this room. Signs of illness will be shown in the form of headaches or kidney problems. Seek medical advice and attention when necessary. Those of you already suffering from complications related to these areas should temporary use another room.

農曆十二月 **(January 5th - February 2nd 2021)** 己丑

Minor illness is expected for those using this room. Although it is just minor problems, it can still be somewhat troublesome. Pay attention to throat ailments, or toothaches and gum infections. It is advisable to get it treated as soon as possible to avoid complications. Communication is at an all-time low this month, so you're likely to be involved in miscommunication and misunderstandings with the people closest to you. It's not a month for love, either, as your new infatuation or romance is likely to lead to scandal, not great happiness!

Northeast Sector Main Door

Northeast Sector Main Door

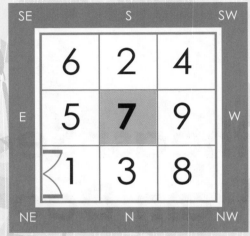

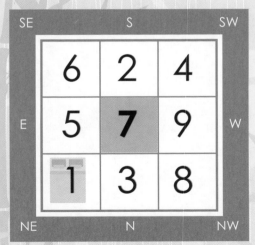

This section contains the monthly outlook for all 12 months of the year for different bedroom sectors in a property with a Northeast Main Door.

SE — S — SW

6	2	4
5	**7**	9
1	3	8

E — W

NE — N — NW

Ground Floor

SE — S — SW

6	2	4
5	**7**	9
1	3	8

E — W

NE — N — NW

First Floor

農曆正月 (February 4th - March 4th) 戊寅

Couples using this room may face some relationship issues concerning jealousy and suspicion. It's time to practice patience and honesty, and be open to your partner. Refrain from involving in speculative investments, especially equity investment and gambling, as there is a likelihood of losses and some may have more serious consequences than expected. It is best to play it safe this month. Health issues regarding breast or liver should be paid attention to as well.

農曆二月 (March 5th - April 3rd) 己卯

Asset investments shall see a rewarding return this month. This is especially true for trading or investments that take place abroad. Both personal and professional relationships progress well. Students using this room will also see positive outcomes academically.

農曆三月 (April 4th - May 4th) 庚辰

Those of you working in the furniture industry will find this an auspicious month. Significant profits and returns are heading your way. However, beware of the backstabber and petty person this month, as betrayal will usually cause loss of wealth and result in legal problems. Avoid trusting people easily. Plans for partnerships and new alliances shall be postponed until a suitable time to avoid the risk of financial loss.

農曆四月 (May 5th - June 4th) 辛巳

Elderly women should avoid using this room, as the risk of falling sick is high. Couples using this room should also be aware of small fights that could develop into serious arguments. However, the good news is that those who involve in the real estate business are likely to be quite profitable under the influence of the energies in the room. Take the chance and make the most out of any potential leads that come up.

Northeast Sector Main Door

農曆五月 (June 5th - July 5th) 壬午

Those using this room should expect heightened media attention, publicity and recognition this month. In a nutshell, be prepared to be in the spotlight! Just make sure you turn the attention and the elevated reputation into a cementing force for your career. Substantial rewards are awaiting as long as you are willing to make changes for the better, or begin anew on certain matters.

農曆六月 (July 6th - August 6th) 癸未

The energies in this room will give a boost in terms of academic results for students who are taking important examinations this month. Your passions are ought to turn into an opportunity for career advancement, particularly for those in the entertainment industry. Don't put a lid on your enthusiasm or you might limit the opportunities available to you. Your talents and abilities are finally recognized by your superior, which could lead to promotion and financial reward. Overall, this month is all-systems-go!

農曆七月 (August 7th - September 6th) 甲申

It's time for those in the oil and gas industries to take advantage of the opportunities that arise this month. Make sure you are alert and quick enough to capitalise on the chance that comes up. Opportunities to shine has come to the salaried employee working on special projects, as the projects in question take off spectacularly. Be prepared to revel in a lot of praise and recognition!

農曆八月 (September 7th - October 7th) 乙酉

Improvements will be seen in communication with family members this month, and you will be able to enjoy closer ties. If you are planning to go on a trip, be sure that your travel insurance is up to date, as there is a chance of mishaps during the trip resulting in possible injuries to the limbs. Beware of the people with whom you share your work, and exercise some form of caution.

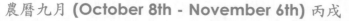

農曆九月 (October 8th - November 6th) 丙戌

In general, this is a good month for networking and making new contacts. If you are in politics career, this is a good time for a politician to push your new policies, as you will likely receive support from your constituents. Career progress and development shall be also seen for those in competitive sports.

農曆十月 (November 7th - December 6th) 丁亥

Those who are already feeling unwell should avoid this room, as there is a chance of worsening the situation. Get a thorough check-up, especially for breast and liver cancer to eliminate the possibility of illness. Refrain from speculative investment, especially equity investments and gambling as there is a risk of financial losses. Plans to be involved in the risk-taking financial plays shall be postponed to another, where the outcomes are less likely to cause huge damage. Couples using this bedroom should communicate more with each other to reduce the damage of suspicion.

農曆十一月 (December 7th 2020 - January 4th 2021) 戊子

Children taking important examinations will benefit from the energies in this room. It will help with the clarity of mind and focus when conducting studies and revision. Assets acquisitions deals concluded this month should perform a rewarding result, especially if these are investments abroad or if you are dealing with overseas contacts.

農曆十二月 (January 5th - February 2nd 2021) 己丑

Refrain from investing in real estate at this point, as it would probably result in losses. Plans for assets acquirement shall be postponed to a more suitable timing. Looking at the domestic relationship, you may find the elder ladies at home behaving more stubbornly. Exercise patience and seek to understand their point of view and dissatisfaction by sitting down and talking to them where possible.

| Main Door | Northeast | Bedroom Sector | North |

農曆正月 (February 4th - March 4th) 戊寅

Avoid using this room for those who already feeling unwell. There is the risk of injuries, and if one does take place then don't ignore the symptoms or resulting consequences. You are likely to see deals from overseas partners or contacts abroad making a good financial profit, however, extra financial control should also take place. This should be adhered to because theft and fraud are likely to take place, especially among people you thought you could trust.

農曆二月 (March 5th - April 3rd) 己卯

Career progressions are likely this month and it comes with an elevation of power, status, and authority. Bear in mind, progressions could also mean the increased of work and responsibilities, so be prepared. Meanwhile, avoid getting into disputes and arguments with your friends, otherwise, legal trouble just might come out of it. Be aware of the tension from early on, and seek to diffuse it.

農曆三月 (April 4th - May 4th) 庚辰

This is not a month to invest your money in speculative investments or gambling activities, as the results are likely to show losses, or in the worst case, leads to a lawsuit. Ensure that you strive to put away your money instead of taking a risk on it. Pay extra care on health issues like ulcers, gallstones and liver problems, and those who live in rural areas may have a problem with unexpected snakebites.

農曆四月 (May 5th - June 4th) 辛巳

Those using this room may encounter some emotional and psychological problems. There shall be no shame in asking for help if you realize something is not right. Talk to someone if you need to. Those involved in research and development will see opportunities to make a name for yourself this month, especially if you are working on a project from an overseas company. Couples should make an effort in your relationship, as there could be competitors on the horizon if you neglect your duties and responsibilities.

農曆五月 (June 5th - July 5th) 壬午

Beware of car accidents this month if you are using this room. Be sure not to drive when you are feeling unwell or exhausted, especially when you need to make long-haul trips. Be careful with your every word and actions, apply common-sense and reason to your commute to divert potential risks. Those wishing to further their political career and who need to rely on oratory skills will likely do well this month.

農曆六月 (July 6th - August 6th) 癸未

You may see a good financial profit from unexpected property deals this month, but be very specific on the details, as legal issues may arise if you are not careful. Consult a lawyer or someone familiar with the legalities when you are in doubt. There may also be problems with the authorities in the form of outstanding taxes and fines, so be sure to clear all outstanding payments before any legal action taken. Relationships are on a downturn, so avoid making any important decision as the results are likely to be less than pleasing.

農曆七月 (August 7th - September 6th) 甲申

This will be a favourable month for those in the construction business, especially if you are required to travel to conclude your deals, as you will see positive outcomes for your hard work. Those who artistically incline, particularly sculptors and carvers, will find a sudden increase in demand in their works. Those in unsettled relationships, both personal and professional, may find yourself at the end of the road this month, which requires you to make a decision that will bring a definite outcome.

農曆八月 (September 7th - October 7th) 乙酉

Beware of rivals attacking you from out of the blue this month, which could even end in a hostile takeover. You will find it is more difficult to find good deals compared to the usual, and you may want to consider concluding previous deals at a later time, as this is not the most suitable time to close deals. Be careful about the potential plaguing of scams and frauds.

農曆九月 (October 8th - November 6th) 丙戌

This is a good month for financial gains. Those in the property and real estate business are likely to make money using their past experiences and superior knowledge to the best advantages. Excellent gains will also be seen for those in the fashion and clothing retail line. However, beware of those who are jealous of your success. It will be best for you to keep a low-profile and stay away from those who seem too overly concerned with your affairs.

農曆十月 (November 7th - December 6th) 丁亥

Those who are already in poor health should avoid this room, as there will be risks of internal injuries this month. Seek professional advice if anything seems amiss. Be sure to assess matters practically and straightforwardly and avoid letting emotions to get in the way of true and authentic evaluation. Windfall gains can be attained from deals made with overseas partners and contacts abroad, however, it is advisable to put extra financial control in place. Beware of theft and fraud issues as well, especially by close friends and family members.

農曆十一月 (December 7th 2020 - January 4th 2021) 戊子

There is a possibility of career advancement in a new position with more power and authority, which usually comes in more responsibility. So be prepared for the onslaught. Male teenagers may need to consider moving into another room as the energies in this room would lead to more rebellious actions. Try your best to diffuse any strong tensions between friends, instead of provoking disputes, to avoid any legal complications.

農曆十二月 (January 5th - February 2nd 2021) 己丑

For those involved in management and consulting, this will be a good month to expand your business. Professionals in the literary and media industry will also do quite well this month in terms of inspiration and productivity. However, couples are likely to experience a tense relationship, which filled with small fight and petty quarrels. Consider going off on a trip and take daily undertakings off of your shoulder, even for a little while, would help in relieving the tension between both of you.

| Main Door | Northeast | Bedroom Sector | Northwest |

農曆正月 (February 4th - March 4th) 戊寅

Young children using this room should be careful with small and sharp metal objects, as the energies in the room portrayed risks of injuries. Monitor them closely and try to keep them off from such implements. Although it seems to be a lot of setbacks in this month, it is important to keep your spirit up to turn negative events into positive outcomes.

農曆二月 (March 5th - April 3rd) 己卯

Your relationship, be it personal or professional will proceed smoothly this month. Effective communications always come after minimal stress. It will make life a breeze on the domestic front, while in the workplace, you will see better engagement between you and your colleagues, superiors and subordinates. If you are in the role of leadership or have some form of power or authority, you can expect to enjoy a very good month indeed. Investments in speculative real-estate will also see positive outcomes this month.

農曆三月 (April 4th - May 4th) 庚辰

Business will see positive outcomes for those in the construction and engineering industries, and good chances to make good investment abroad is available, even if it means traveling far and away from your current business. Previous investments are likely to see positive outcomes, especially for fund and investment managers. Couples using this room are blessed to have a harmonious and rewarding relationship this month.

農曆四月 (May 5th - June 4th) 辛巳

Couples using this room are likely to receive good news if you wished to start a family. You will find recognition comes to you when you have excelled in your specific field, or for something in which that you have been specifically involved and have helped drive to its conclusion. This will bring about some moments of pleasure as the others come to recognize and appreciate your talents and achievements. Those in the travel or construction industry will see a pleasant improvement in profits.

| Main Door | Northeast | Bedroom Sector | Northwest |

農曆五月 (June 5th - July 5th) 壬午

Profits are possible this month but it may take some extra effort to conclude these deals. If you need to put in extra hours to help matter along further, then you should be willing to make the appropriate sacrifice as the rewards will be immense. This is also a good month for new partnerships. As for employees who want to make a breakthrough, you will need to find out what are the obstacles and seek to dissolve it.

農曆六月 (July 6th - August 6th) 癸未

Windfall gains are possible this month, so look to realize these profits in your portfolio. If you are in the share and equity markets, you will see a good profit if you cash in your shares. However, you will need to work on financial control this month instead of letting the money slip through your fingers. This is also a good month for networking and developing new client and business relationships, just put your best foot forward and engage your diplomatic skill, the outcomes will be better than you expected. Children using this room are likely to see positive academic results; while couples will enjoy a blissful and harmonious month.

農曆七月 (August 7th - September 6th) 甲申

Good financial profits are possible for deals that require you to travel to conclude, so persist in finalizing the deals abroad if possible. Any form of travel abroad is likely to bring a distinctive new business, which could result in increased profit for our business. Family businesses will see prosperity. Those working in the banking industry can look forward to a promotion or career advancement this month; while those in futures, share and equity trading business will also do well this month.

農曆八月 (September 7th - October 7th) 乙酉

Wealth fortunes are generally in favour of those using this room this month. Couples using this room will find the increased quality of relationship, and fulfillment can be derived from your ties. Employees may experience higher stress levels than the previous month as superiors are more likely to step up the pressure for you to perform. Learn how to cope with high expectations, manage anxiety and turn it into useful energy.

農曆九月 (October 8th - November 6th) 丙戌

Deals which requires you to travel to conclude are usually more lucrative, such as overseas deals or clients from overseas companies. Students taking important examinations are likely to see positive outcomes using this room this month, as it is generally a good sector to help you focus your energy and develop your level of concentration.

農曆十月 (November 7th - December 6th) 丁亥

It is a rather difficult month but things can be turned around into a positive situation by making some key changes. Your thoughts may be clouded by the troubles you face, but try to seek advice from others to help you think clearly. Young children should avoid using this room this month, as there are risks of injuries by sharp implements. At best, keep sharp metal objects out of their reach.

農曆十一月 (December 7th 2020 - January 4th 2021) 戊子

You will see a better turn of fortune this month. Thick profits from speculative investments in real estate are likely to be seen, but be sure that the details are taken care of by lawyers. Relationships will tend to be smooth sailing with no stress or tension, as communication problems will melt away. Things are in your favour this month be sure to grab any opportunity that comes your way. It will allow you to exercise your rule and display your leadership skills.

農曆十二月 (January 5th - February 2nd 2021) 己丑

The elderly folks or those already in poor health should avoid using this room, as the energies in the room this month doesn't bode well with and would only further aggravate their health issues. Liver problems, in particular, would be a significant concern. For those in the education industry, beware of intense competition from industrial rivals. The good news is that you will find profits from your endeavours as long as you execute your business plans carefully and with shrewdness. Females in the marketing and public relations business using this room will find immense benefits coming to them at work.

Main Door	Northeast	Bedroom Sector	West

農曆正月 (February 4th - March 4th) 戊寅

Salaried employees will find their employer's expectation increased tenfold this month. It may be somewhat difficult to deal with their demands, yet all you can do is to try to fulfill them to the best of your ability. If however, you find that the workload is too much to cope with, voice out to your superiors and try to find a middle ground that works for everyone.

農曆二月 (March 5th - April 3rd) 己卯

Promotions and profits are likely this month for those working in engineering, or the travel industry. Be bold to request for that promotion if that is what you want. The singles using this room will find it an ideal month for romance, so you may want to take advantage of the situation and ask out the person you've had an eye on for some time.

農曆三月 (April 4th - May 4th) 庚辰

This will be a very good month, in terms of career development, for people using this room. Those who are self-employed or own businesses will be able to enjoy an enhanced reputation, while for salaried employees, there are strong chances for a promotion. Personal relationships will also do well this month, so take advantage of the positive energies and make an effort to forge closer ties with your loved ones.

農曆四月 (May 5th - June 4th) 辛巳

This is a favourable month for self-improvement, as attempts at self-cultivation will be fruitful and leave you feeling satisfied. Embarking on a new program for a living, or take up meditation and other soul-replenishing activities are likely to see desirable outcomes. Important decisions that had been holding off can finally conclude, as clarity of thought is at its unvarnished prime this month. Health is generally good, but be sure that there are no negative features located outside this sector.

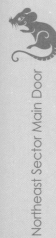

| Main Door | Northeast | Bedroom Sector | West |

農曆五月 (June 5th - July 5th) 壬午

Those using this room are likely to celebrate some good news this month. Married couples may be able to welcome a new member in their life. Those who are in a committed relationship should be able to go forth and pop the question – and receive the desired answer. Positive results are possible to reflect on property investments, as finances are all looking quite rosy this month.

農曆六月 (July 6th - August 6th) 癸未

Bad temper proves to be a concerning-issue this month, as the negative energies in this room will leave an unpleasing effect on your emotions. This might lead you to be very anti-social, and you will find it difficult to get along with others. However, don't fret over as things will blow over soon. Those in a relationship should give more space to your partner, and make sure not to influence each other with bad energies and temper.

農曆七月 (August 7th - September 6th) 甲申

You may experience opposition and questions to your authority from rebellious subordinates and employees. Try to figure out the reason behind this, as they are most likely disgruntled over issues that prove to be quite significant. It would be best to show compassion, instead of showing heavy-headed authority. This way, troubles will be solved easily and everyone can move on.

農曆八月 (September 7th - October 7th) 乙酉

Health issues should be paid extra attention this month. Refrain from having any negative structure placed outside of this sector to avoid any stomach and digestive problems, particularly the risk of food poisoning. If you are not carefully, it is likely to lead to discomfort in the stomach and digestive problems, even if it is not serious. Financial loss rather than gains are likely to be the norm of this month; therefore, it is better to stick to conservative investments.

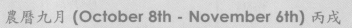

農曆九月 (October 8th - November 6th) 丙戌

As you will only receive minimal support for your ideas and projects this month, you'll find it is rather difficult and hard to overcome obstacles at work. Avoid starting any important or major projects this month. It will be better to keep a low profile and do your planning at this stage, conserving your energy and productivity for a more fruitful time in the future.

農曆十月 (November 7th - December 6th) 丁亥

Works tend to be a little demanding this month, and you may need to juggle multiple projects to please your superior. If things become overwhelming, do not hesitate to voice out and ask for help. Be sure do proper arrangement and planning on the priorities to ensure your workflow is well-organized.

農曆十一月 (December 7th 2020 - January 4th 2021) 戊子

The positive energies in the room bode well with the romantic vibes this month. Those who are in committed relationships, you will see a good progression in your relationship with very little effort on your part. For the singles, it's time to step up the pace or make a move and ask your crush out. Those working in the engineering and travel business should be bold and ask for a promotion, as results are likely to be good.

農曆十二月 (January 5th - February 2nd 2021) 己丑

Expectant mothers should consider moving into another room this month, as there will be risks of miscarriage if continues staying in this room. For married couples, beware of third-party gossip causing you some amount of tension in your relationship. Guard against unreasonable jealousy, which will cause a certain amount of problems. Those working in the real estate business will see thick profits from property deals.

農曆正月 (February 4th - March 4th) 戊寅

In general, this would be a favourable month, especially for those involved in the real estate and property business. It is possible to see a marked increase in stature as a promotion or likely recognition comes your way, and profits are likely to come from the property market. Those using this room should consider joint ventures, as it would benefit you greatly.

農曆二月 (March 5th - April 3rd) 己卯

Those of you working in hazardous environment will need to be extra cautious this month, as there is a potential risk of injuries from sharp objects and machinery. Scrutinize and examine all the fine prints and details when signing legal documents to avoid potential fraud and cheating. Pay attention to what you say and watch your words, especially those using this room, to avoid end up hurting, offending or angering someone with your speech.

農曆三月 (April 4th - May 4th) 庚辰

This would be a beneficial month to build on your personal and professional relationship, as improvements are likely this month. So, work on your relationship and enjoy closer ties with people around. However, you will need to be more careful and forethought about speculative investments in equity, shares and futures and keep them to a minimum, as losses are possible this month. You are most likely to see improvement in your stature, reputation and name if you travel to conduct business, so strive to make as many business opportunities abroad.

農曆四月 (May 5th - June 4th) 辛巳

This is a month to play it safe and stick to the rules. Those involved in speculative investments, especially property or real estate, should withdraw from their deals before losses are experienced. Gambling activities should also be avoided as it may end in financial losses. Females are likely to experience health issues this month. It is best to get a medical checkup and mammogram to eliminate all possibilities and risks of illness. Do not put any sign of illness off to another time if you already sense of feeling that something is amiss.

| Main Door | Northeast | Bedroom Sector | Southwest |

農曆五月 (June 5th - July 5th) 壬午

Those having problems with asthma and bronchitis should pay extra attention if using this bedroom. It is best to take any precautionary methods if necessary. See your doctor if symptoms seem more pronounced than usual to rule out any unnecessary complications. Refrain from any gambling activities as you may need to stand to endure heavy losses. Just like the previous month, it is best to play it safe and stick to the rules.

農曆六月 (July 6th - August 6th) 癸未

Parents should pay more attention to your children, as they may get involved in rebellious activities encouraged by peer pressure. Those who are artistically creative will find high demand for your work and people are more willing to pay for good creative work. Those traveling this month should expect some sudden change that makes necessitate the purchase of travel insurance.

農曆七月 (August 7th - September 6th) 甲申

This is a good month to invest in self-cultivation and self-development, either by attending new courses or learning a new trade. If meditation and reading are your interest, this will be a good room to use. Fortune is in favour of especially female employees this month. Those of you in the real estate industry will see increased turnover as well. However, there will be problems with the in-laws this month, and it is best to keep contact at a minimal level or practice tolerance and patience in your outlook.

農曆八月 (September 7th - October 7th) 乙酉

This will be a good time for authors and journalists to look for new publishers if you wished to release new publications. Those in the art and culture industry using this room will receive media attention and publicity. You can expect to prepare for your moment in the spotlight. Students should tap into the energies of this bedroom as the academic luck is strong this month, so take advantage of the positive vibes if you are facing important examinations. The energies in this room also bode well with building alliance partners abroad and embarking business expansion.

農曆九月 (October 8th - November 6th) 丙戌

This is the month for you to go forth and seal the deal, as it is likely to benefit from the lucrative investment opportunities available. You should take full advantage of the upswing relationship this month and make sure that you spend more time with your spouse or partner and with your loved ones. It will benefit you as it will develop closer ties between you and your loved ones. However, it is not a good time to travel, as there will be obstacles made by your rivals into your client base while you are away.

農曆十月 (November 7th - December 6th) 丁亥

Those using this room are likely to find an increase in status and authority. Those involved in the property and real estate business can expect promotion, recognition and advancement this month. Energies this month also bodes well in joint ventures. If this is your line, then it is suitable to get involved in gilt bonds or shares. You may want to pay extra attention to health issues, especially aching at the back and spine injuries.

農曆十一月 (December 7th 2020 - January 4th 2021) 戊子

Those in the furniture industry are most likely to do well this month, however, be sure to be extra careful when signing legal documents, as overlooking some details may lead to legal complications. Pay attention to the fine print and consult a lawyer when you are in doubt. Be sure to watch your words this month, as your words might come back to haunt you or you may easily be misunderstood. It is best for you to watch your speech and to think carefully before you express yourself.

農曆十二月 (January 5th - February 2nd 2021) 己丑

Refrain from giving personal loans this month, especially to relatives and family members, as you might not see the money again. Parents should pay more attention to your children, as they are likely to be more rebellious and difficult to control or discipline this month. The good news is that those involved in the legal or arbitration business will be enjoying their fruit of labour with the proper amount of effort put in.

Main Door	Northeast	Bedroom Sector	South

農曆正月 (February 4th - March 4th) 戊寅

Elderly women using this room are likely to face potential risks of abdominal illness. Pay attention to any sign of illness and don't put off a medical consultation for too long. It will be best to consult your doctor at the early sign of discomfort. Be sure to check all legal documents thoroughly and scrutinize the fine prints before dropping your signature on the dotted line, because all legal dealings are fraught with potential risks at this point. This is especially true for those of you working or involved in finance and trading.

農曆二月 (March 5th - April 3rd) 己卯

Generally, those in the literary field and publishing will find potential success this month, especially women. The likelihood of rewards and achievements and an increase in your reputation and stature is high. Be ready to let the good time roll and allow yourself to feel good for being in the center of attention. However, the in-laws may find themselves in odd this month, so it is best to keep a distance from each other to avoid triggering disputes and arguments. It is also a good month to work on self-improvement.

農曆三月 (April 4th - May 4th) 庚辰

Those involved in religious or spiritual endeavours will find this a good month to tap into the energies of this room, as it is conducive for peaceful thought and reflection. Be sure that you had cleared all your taxes and fines, or you may find yourself in trouble with the law. Couples should give each other some space and consider keeping distance, as sharing this room may lead to a tense and stressed relationship. Keeping distance with each other allows both of you to deal with your stress and problems.

農曆四月 (May 5th - June 4th) 辛巳

You will see profitable returns and a great demand for your skills for those in the medical field. Your reputation and stature are likely to see a boost and you will be able to enjoy some welcome accolades. Investments in property deals are likely to receive a quick and favourable return. Expectant mothers should avoid this room, as the chance of miscarriage is possible.

Main Door	Northeast	Bedroom Sector	South

農曆五月 (June 5th - July 5th) 壬午

Be sure to exercise caution and control your spending even though your financial luck is somewhat good this month. There is no need to make lavish purchases solely to display extravagant forms of generosity. It is best to avoid arguments with your friends and family, as maintaining good ties with them is a better choice of move. Try not to be too trusting this month as people are likely to take advantage of you, and the more you are willing to hedge around and give them room, the bolder they will become.

農曆六月 (July 6th - August 6th) 癸未

Refrain from making any important decisions this month, as your decisions are likely to be clouded by confusion, resulting in making poor choices. Be mindful of the way you interact with your family members to avoid family disharmony and arguments. Expectant mothers should consider moving into another room this month, for there is a possibility of miscarriage or pregnancy complications if continue using this room. Be sure to take all proper precautions to eliminate diseases at its earliest stage.

農曆七月 (August 7th - September 6th) 甲申

For those using this room should beware of health issues like gastric and intestinal problems. There will be several emotional setbacks this month triggered by paranoia and superstition. Try your best to focus on emotional strength despite the negative feelings. It is better to share your problem and talk to people when necessary to help yourself get a better grasp on the situation.

農曆八月 (September 7th - October 7th) 乙酉

Side investments are likely to return good profits this month. If you make smart decisions, you can expect to enjoy a well-padded wallet! For the doctors, you will find that your skills are in great demand, and will see increased business. Couples using this room will see difficulties on conception. If possible, try shifting to another room.

農曆九月 (October 8th - November 6th) 丙戌

Those involved in religious pursuits or those gaining spiritual knowledge should use this bedroom this month, as it is conducive for those types of activities. Employees will find their efforts don't return in a desirable result, especially an equal amount of fruit of labour. Don't let this get you down. Avoid focusing too much on the result, instead, use your level of personal satisfaction as your benchmark.

農曆十月 (November 7th - December 6th) 丁亥

Be sure to exercise extreme caution when signing legal documents and in all legal dealings, as the possibilities of fraud and cheating may occur. Financial loss is possible this month, especially for those directly involved in the finance sector, so take some necessary steps and avoid being ignorant to mitigate the risk of losses. Elder women using this room should pay attention to abdominal illness this month.

農曆十一月 (December 7th 2020 - January 4th 2021) 戊子

Women in the literary field will see to receive awards and achievements. Be ready to shine bright in the spotlight! The energies of room benefit self-cultivation activities this month, so if opportunities arise, be sure take up a self-development course. The relationship of the in-laws are likely to be tense, so some patience will go a long way this month. If you're either one of the above, it will be best to exercise tact and diplomacy in your dealings with the others.

農曆十二月 (January 5th - February 2nd 2021) 己丑

Most people using this room will find this a profitable month, but those in the construction field are especially favoured by the energies of this room. Yielding of positive outcomes are likely from business trips, so be sure to take the chance and embark on every possible journey. It is best to eliminate any negative formations outside of this room to avoid health issues like liver-related problems. Be sure to seek immediate treatment at the first sign of unwell. Couples using this room are more likely to experience a sensitive relationship. Care for the emotions of each other, be more tactful and sensitive in your daily interaction, and avoid taking each other for granted.

| Main Door | Northeast | Bedroom Sector | Southeast |

農曆正月 (February 4th - March 4th) 戊寅

Those using this room and experiencing a rocky relationship or a floundering business partnership are most likely to face the end of the tie. However, this is not necessarily a bad thing because it will eventually lead to an auspicious new beginning. Couples are likely to find themselves going through a rough patch with each other. Be sure to take extra care of the manner of speech and behavior. Those of you in the spa and tourism business will benefit from travelling because it will help lead you to new business prospects and contacts.

農曆二月 (March 5th - April 3rd) 己卯

Elderly males using this room need to take extra care of their health, especially problems with blood pressure and lung diseases. Children are likely to be more rebellious and stubborn this month. Parents should deal with it calmly, as that would help in defusing the tension. At work front, it is best to stay away from office politics.

農曆三月 (April 4th - May 4th) 庚辰

Career advancement in terms of a change in career or a salary raise is likely this month, and this could result in favourable financial rewards. This month offers a good financial return for investment and merchant bankers who engage in stock and corporate deals. It is more likely to achieve financial success if you can take in the advice and suggestion provided by coaches and mentors around you.

農曆四月 (May 5th - June 4th) 辛巳

Physical fights and legal complications may occur due to jealousy and rivalry among males. It is better to put the bravado aside and consider the situation using reasons. This is a month for short-term flings rather than long term relationships, so avoid putting too much expectation into any new relationship formed.

| Main Door | Northeast | Bedroom Sector | Southeast |

農曆五月 (June 5th - July 5th) 壬午

Employers are likely to find their employees to be rather rebellious and hard to handle this month. Good profits are possible but a more hands-on approach is required to maximize profits. Getting involved in your business can also help you to determine where is the financial leak and losses occur. This bedroom is beneficial to those into professional sports and is participating in any competitive event.

農曆六月 (July 6th - August 6th) 癸未

Relationship with family members seems to be tense and strained. It is better just to keep the peace, as this is not a good time to thrash it out with the family. Labour relationship is likely to play a big role this month, so beware of any arising law challenges related to the sacking of staff and employees. Return profits from property investments are possible but it will require a good knowledge of the market to be successful in the venture.

農曆七月 (August 7th - September 6th) 甲申

New ideas and inspiration will find its way to those in the academic and literary fields, which are likely to bring favourable financial gains. Academic results of children are most likely to be favourable if they use this room to prepare for examinations. Those involved in the psychological, counseling or mentor field will find their skills greatly sought after, which could lead to gaining respects, earning recognition and raise of reputation. This is a good month for those who wish to use travel as a means of producing more income.

農曆八月 (September 7th - October 7th) 乙酉

There could be leg injuries caused by travel-related problems this month, so be especially careful on any of your travel trips. Minor health issues may occur but it is advisable not to ignore or think that these are not important or it could end up as more serious conditions that would cause more trouble and treatment cost further down the road. Be careful when driving and out and about, as there is an increased risk of car accidents and injuries. Employees in the engineering field will find their superiors are rather supportive this month, which could result in financial rewards and recognition.

農曆九月 (October 8th - November 6th) 丙戌

Those in the spiritual or metaphysical development field are encouraged to tap into the energies of this room, as both bode well together and allow those using the room to have a clear mind and good concentration to focus on meditation and reflection. Obstructions may be in the way in career prospects for salaried employees. Be patient and wait it out, it is only temporary. Women using this room should get themselves a thorough medical check-up to eliminate any possible diseases, especially gynaecological problems.

農曆十月 (November 7th - December 6th) 丁亥

This month, the energies in this room bode well with those who wanted a new start. Entrepreneur and those wishing to embark on new ventures should tap into these auspicious vibes to ensure a smooth sailing new beginning. A rocky relationship or business partnership that is on the verge of a break up will be exacerbated if this room is used this month. It is time to take extra care in your dealings with your partner, in terms of both personal and professional relationships.

農曆十一月 (December 7th 2020 - January 4th 2021) 戊子

Parents will find their children who use this room acting more rebellious and hard to control this month. Be sure to find a way to manage the rebelliousness, or it might be a difficult future ahead. It is advisable to keep out of the office politics and maintain a low profile at work, as there may be internal bickering this month. Elderly males should pay extra attention to their health, especially with problems regarding high blood pressure or lung diseases.

農曆十二月 (January 5th - February 2nd 2021) 己丑

Communication is found to be at an all-time low, and misunderstandings abound. As such, couples need to be more sensitive and patient with each other's emotions and needs. At work front, be sure to communicate coherently, otherwise, you risk your words being misunderstood or misinterpreted, and lead to more serious troubles. Certain niggling health problems also come to the fore this month. Make sure to get plenty of rest, sufficient water intake, and watch out for any possible throat ailments.

Main Door	Northeast	Bedroom Sector	East

農曆正月 (February 4th - March 4th) 戊寅

Business networks may seem to dwindle this month. It is best to adapt by learning some necessary skills so that you are well-equipped should the need arise. Romantic relationship may experience some pressure and stress due to constant arguments and fights. Practice patience and be more understanding of each other. Watch out for health issues related to ears and kidneys.

農曆二月 (March 5th - April 3rd) 己卯

For business owners, it is advisable not to focus or execute expansion and growth. Instead, use this time to consolidate your current interests and to brainstorm for future strategies. Special attention should be paid to your customers and clients as well. Take necessary steps to ensure that no unsatisfied employees are being treacherous behind your back. Financial wealth is likely to come from modest and conservative property deals.

農曆三月 (April 4th - May 4th) 庚辰

Those using this room are likely to be affected by competition and rivalry from the competitors. This will probably become a very emotional issue and result in psychological warfare. It is good to keep your guard up, but there is no need to overact and resort to petty responses. Lawyers will find it difficult to put their case across this month, so it is better to postpone cases to a more favourable period. Muscle and tendon injuries are possible due to accidents caused by mishaps with other people.

農曆四月 (May 5th - June 4th) 辛巳

Those involved in the professional sports field will find themselves going through an uphill battle this month, and should instead use this time to make some physical improvements that can bring future benefits. Health issues like migraines and headaches may also arise, so try to relax more and not let worries and anxieties get the best of you.

Main Door	Northeast	Bedroom Sector	East

農曆五月 (June 5th - July 5th) 壬午

Those who are in the fashion and apparel industries, brace yourself for a rather disastrous period this month. It is best to keep a low profile and stay away from any possible disputes or arguments. For business owners, be forewarned that things could go wrong, even those that usually run smoothly, will end up in troubles and obstructions. Expectant mothers should avoid this room at all costs, as using it may result in pregnancy complications.

農曆六月 (July 6th - August 6th) 癸未

Refrain from making speculative investment and gambling this month, as it is likely to cause financial losses. You will find problems arising this month will be hard to solve, as the cause is not easily evident. Beware of your rivals, as they would take quick advantage of this factor. Stay away from casual relationships this month, as the risk of sexually transmitted diseases is likely.

農曆七月 (August 7th - September 6th) 甲申

This is a favourable month for the lawyers and those in dispute resolution business, as this is a month of petty disputes and conflicts resulting in harmful results and lingering problems. Avoid lending money to anyone this month, especially to family members, unless you never want to see your money again. Males using this room will find themselves entangled in lawsuits arising out of car accidents.

農曆八月 (September 7th - October 7th) 乙酉

Be sure to eliminate any negative structure outside of this room, as it would leave bad effects and trigger unforeseen illness or accidents. Mothers and older women should avoid this room, as increased risks of kidney problems and related ailments are likely. Refrain from making any property acquisition this month, for it will likely to end in failure.

農曆九月 (October 8th - November 6th) 丙戌

Health should be your top concern this month, especially with bladder and kidney problems. Business partners should be aware of possible fallout from stress and tension, as it could result in loss of wealth. It is advisable to settle lawsuits out of court or it may end up costing a lot more for all involved.

農曆十月 (November 7th - December 6th) 丁亥

You may find minimal support from mentors and superiors this month, and as a result, you may see business contract drying up. You will need to learn and equip the necessary skills quickly to manage the matter that arises. Couples should consider using another, as the energies in this room may cause disputes and fights. Pay extra attention to your health issue, especially with the ears and kidneys.

農曆十一月 (December 7th 2020 - January 4th 2021) 戊子

Good financial gains are likely to be seen in conservative property related deals, however, businesses will lack the leverage to benefit from positive investment outcomes. Expansion of business shall be avoided this month, and instead, focus on consolidating the existing business. Pay extra attention to customers and clients, as there may be disloyalty among employees, which leads to sabotaging your enterprise or company by leaking unwanted information towards your customer base.

農曆十二月 (January 5th - February 2nd 2021) 己丑

Refrain from getting involved in office politics this month, as it could result in legal complications if blown out of proportion. It is best to focus on your job and ignore all the rivals or backstabbers at work. You will eventually find that the rewards are a lot more fulfilling than being caught up in office politics. Financial gains are possible for those actively involved in the stocks and shares trading. Seek advice from more seasoned investors when you are unsure about how to proceed.

West Sector
Main Door

Main Door	West	Bedroom Sector	West

This section contains the monthly outlook for all 12 months of the year, for different bedroom sectors in a property with a West Main Door.

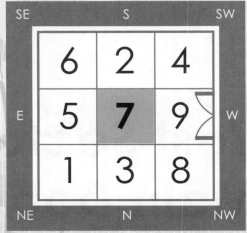

Ground Floor

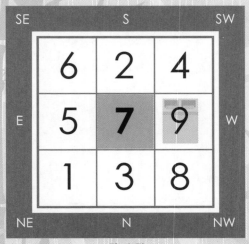

First Floor

農曆正月 (February 4th - March 4th) 戊寅

Relationships will see a significant improvement this month for those using this room. The energies in this room also bode well for scholarly activities, so students who are going to sit for important examinations should take advantage of the positive vibe in this room throughout the month.

農曆二月 (March 5th - April 3rd) 己卯

Those of you in the fashion business will find the need to travel to conclude major deal. On a positive note, this could bring better profit as a result. The payoff will be worth it, so don't hesitate to put in your effort even if it creates a more hectic schedule. Meditations and self-development endeavours are likely to bring beneficial outcome in this room, as the energies in this room favours spiritual and religious activities.

農曆三月 (April 4th - May 4th) 庚辰

Good news and celebration are in store for politicians and civil servants. You will find your status and position elevated, as a result of your tireless efforts. Be sure that you do your best to improve your professional reputation with consistent work. It is also a good time to divest some of the properties under your investment portfolio and cash-in on your investment. Favourable profits are likely to find their way to you.

農曆四月 (May 5th - June 4th) 辛巳

Communication is found to be at an all-time low, and misunderstandings abound. Be sure to communicate coherently, and keep a low profile to avoid troubles. However, models, actors and actresses and those involved in the dramatic arts are likely to receive good publicity from the mass media this month and it would be a perfect time to use it to your advantage.

| Main Door | West | Bedroom Sector | West |

農曆五月 (June 5th - July 5th) 壬午

Those who have invested in metal trading, futures, equities, and stock will find this month profitable, however, you will need to keep abreast of current market trends to capitalise on any favourable situations that may arise. Changes in the workplace, in terms of staff transfers, can be expected as well. Females in the household should take pay extra attention to eye and heart-related ailments this month.

農曆六月 (July 6th - August 6th) 癸未

You may find yourself feeling stressed and under pressure this month, so it would be a good idea to postpone any important decision-making, as your mental faculties aren't functioning at their best. Be vigilant and mindful of any fraudulent activities that could cause you legal problems as well. This is a time to be extremely cautious in handling monetary and financial issues, as disputes over money are very likely during this month.

農曆七月 (August 7th - September 6th) 甲申

Substantial profits are likely through business and network expansions. Take this opportunity to get in touch with all your old friends and associates. You will also find positive media attention for your business expansion, which further enhances your reputation and status. On the home front, be mindful of tension in your relationships, especially where ladies of the household are concerned.

農曆八月 (September 7th - October 7th) 乙酉

Legal issues are possible this month, so be sure to seek advice from your mentors and experienced seniors to work out an amicable solution to your woes. Watch out for any minor ailments. Get them treated once early sign shows up to avoid it escalating into something more serious. You'll be pleased to know that the ability to make money from your investments and the wisdom to invest your gains wisely will benefit you.

農曆九月 (October 8th - November 6th) 丙戌

Peach Blossom luck is in your favour this month. It's time to take your relationships to the next level or to seek out a potential partner. Those working in the engineering and technical field may see an opportunity for promotion this month, so make an appointment with your superior and present your case for a promotion – it is most likely to go well. Those who are feeling unwell should be mindful of cardiac and eye issues this month.

農曆十月 (November 7th - December 6th) 丁亥

The energies in this room are beneficial for academic and scholarly pursuits this month. You will most likely find plenty of opportunities to be recognised and rewarded, in terms of better perks and a possible promotion at work. This should be the time to further consolidate your ties with your partner, as relationships tend to be harmonious and thriving at this point.

農曆十一月 (December 7th 2020 - January 4th 2021) 戊子

You will find your thoughts coherent and clear, and that you are able to make good decisions this month. So, take advantage of this period of time to generate more gains from your investment portfolio and make long-term decisions. All major decisions are best to be made now, when your thoughts and judgment are unclouded.

農曆十二月 (January 5th - February 2nd 2021) 己丑

Elderly women who are feeling unwell should refrain from using this room as much as possible. It is better to move into another room as there is high risk of health issues for those using this room. Couples should avoid picking fights over small issues, or it could result in serious arguments. Those in the real estate business are likely to see good profits this month.

| Main Door | West | Bedroom Sector | Southwest |

農曆正月 (February 4th - March 4th) 戊寅

For those involved in speculative investments, especially property or real estate dealings, it is advisable to pull out early before the market takes a plunge and burns a hole in their bank account. It is not an ideal month to take financial risk, as the fall-out is probably to be quite significant. It is best to stay low profile for the time being.

農曆二月 (March 5th - April 3rd) 己卯

Personal relationship is rather hard-going and requires more effort to maintain a good tie. It is advisable to spend more time with each other, and don't bring your work-related stress home, or allow individual family obligations and problems to take over. However, artists will find this a favourable month to receive a boost for your portfolio and reputation.

農曆三月 (April 4th - May 4th) 庚辰

Couples will see to experience tense relationship this month. It is more likely to affect the women compared to the men, so be sure to practice tolerance and patience when dealing with your partner. Remember to watch your word, don't indulge in verbal swordplay simply to be the one to "win". Indeed, many individuals are probably going to face issues like unhealthy rivalry and deceit, especially those involved in the literary field.

農曆四月 (May 5th - June 4th) 辛巳

The searching for funding and potential sponsors are likely going to show a positive outcome this month for journalists and astronomers. You're also advised to change your property portfolio this month, as you'll stand to reap the rewards of doing so, especially if your investment managers are women. Pay extra attention to internal organs ailments. Elderly women should also consult the doctor, at first sign of pain or discomfort.

| Main Door | West | Bedroom Sector | Southwest |

農曆五月 (June 5th - July 5th) 壬午

It is proven that the scholar and students are likely to benefit from the positive energies of this room this month. Relationship will see to blossom and thrive, more so if there is no water feature in the room. Due to the positive publicity and media attention receive this month, those in the arts and culture industries will also see fame and recognition come rolling.

農曆六月 (July 6th - August 6th) 癸未

Specialists in the metaphysical and services industries are likely to benefit from this room, as long as they are not required to travel to generate their income, as traveling in any form will only result in reduced revenues for them. This is a good month to finalize business deals, as the outcome will probably be in your favour. Establishing a joint-venture and identifying a suitable partner will also see a positive result.

農曆七月 (August 7th - September 6th) 甲申

Elderly or ailment folk should refrain from using this room to avoid the risk of stroke or arterial blockage. It is advisable to get a thorough medical checkup as soon as possible. Married couples will find it a rocky month of relationship. It is especially important to exercise patience and tolerance in dealing with each other.

農曆八月 (September 7th - October 7th) 乙酉

Safety should at the top of your priorities this month, especially if you are required to work with sharp instruments of knives on a regular or daily basis. If you had already been feeling ill, you will need to guard against lung diseases this month. Be sure to see your doctor at the first sign of a cough or wheezing. It is best to avoid disputes and arguments among women, as it could lead to undesirable consequences, or at worst case, a lawsuit at the end of the day.

農曆九月 (October 8th - November 6th) 丙戌

Politicians or civil servants should be mindful when it comes to matters involving real estate, as serious disputes are possible. This is a favourable time to travel to conclude deals, as traveling is likely to bring greater repute, status, and fortune. Likewise, athletes traveling to participate in competitions will also see better results than the others.

農曆十月 (November 7th - December 6th) 丁亥

Ladies of the household should get an immediate medical check-up as soon as possible, as risks of skin problems or breast malignancies are possible. This is not a good month to indulge in gambling activities unless you wish to end up incurring massive financial losses by succumbing to your urges. Financial risk-taking is very unlikely to go down well this month.

農曆十一月 (December 7th 2020 - January 4th 2021) 戊子

Artists and those artistically-inclined should consider publicize your skills at an exhibition of possible, or at least to draw attention to your creative output, as the time is ripe to do so. Likewise, the energies this month bode well for those specializing in the car or auto accessories business to market their products and services. However, couples will need to put a little extra effort into their relationship to maintain good ties and harmony at home.

農曆十二月 (January 5th - February 2nd 2021) 己丑

Refrain from having any negative external formations outside of this room, as there will be risks of mental instability or neurosis caused by stress and depression. Migraines and headaches may arise as health concerns this month, so try to relax more and not let worries and anxieties get the best of you. Those of you who play sports for a living and compete professionally will see yourself going through an uphill battle. Try to take a step back and use the time for some physical improvement that can bring future benefits.

農曆正月 (February 4th - March 4th) 戊寅

It is the month to best exercise patience and tolerance to your partner, for couples who use this room. It is better to leave things to be instead of forcing issues and arguments. Be sure to obey laws and rules, get all your outstanding fines and penalties settled and be on the right side of the law to avoid legal complications.

農曆二月 (March 5th - April 3rd) 己卯

Investments in real estate and property industries are likely to see great returns this month. Overall, this month is filled with a thriving atmosphere. However, those who already feeling unwell should take precautions when using this room, as the energies here could exacerbate illnesses and symptoms.

農曆三月 (April 4th - May 4th) 庚辰

Professional athletes are likely to perform better this month, especially if the events require you to travel. Watch out when you are on the road, as risks of car accidents are possible as well. Expectant mothers using this room should go for a full medical check-up to avoid running into any pregnancy complications.

農曆四月 (May 5th - June 4th) 辛巳

Be forewarned that this will be a rather difficult and hazardous month. Avoid having any negative features outside of this room. Pay extra attention to your physical health, especially the eyes, and your mental health. It is best to find a way to manage your stress level. As your thoughts will tend to be clouded this month, it would be wiser to leave all negotiations and decision-making to a more favourable time.

| Main Door | West | Bedroom Sector | South |

農曆五月 (June 5th - July 5th) 壬午

Those shrewd enough to invest in viable properties or real estate are probably going to see handsome financial profit this month. In fact, there will be plenty of opportunities to improve your fortunes and financial standing. However, refrain from using this room if you are already feeling unwell to avoid further health complications.

農曆六月 (July 6th - August 6th) 癸未

There will be a high possibility of windfall gains this month, so a small gamble or the occasional lottery ticket may bring you some financial gains. However, just be careful not to get carried away or overspend. On the work-front, arguments and jealousy may occur, and it would be advisable for women to stay away from such dispute, as these will mostly lead to disastrous endings.

農曆七月 (August 7th - September 6th) 甲申

Employers are advised to communicate coherently and tactfully with their employees, to eliminate the risk of running into any legal complications. As for businesspersons, be sure that any deals sketched this month doesn't require too much capital, as the financial losses may occur if the risks are high. Legal practitioners and professionals are most likely to find their skills are highly sought-after this month.

農曆八月 (September 7th - October 7th) 乙酉

Pregnant ladies should avoid using this room and all others should watch out for potential appendicitis. Refrain from concluding any business deals or investments this month, as you may find yourself on the losing end. Couples should always remind themselves to exercise tolerance and patience to each other so that disagreements do not get out of hand.

農曆九月 (October 8th - November 6th) 丙戌

You may want to consider moving the ladies in the house to another room, as there may be an occurrence of head-on struggles situation between the ladies. However, the energies this room favour self-cultivation and development pursuits, so be sure to tap into these energies if you seek self-growth. Academics, scholars, and candidates should use this room this month, as they are most probably going to do well in examinations.

農曆十月 (November 7th - December 6th) 丁亥

Make sure all your outstanding fines, summonses, and taxes are settled so that the long arm of the law doesn't catch up with you. Arguments, gossips, and backstabbing will see to be rampant at the workplace this month, so it is advisable to stay out of office politics at all costs. Couples should give each other some breathing space, to minimize the risk of running into any unnecessary arguments or quarrels that may affect their relationship.

農曆十一月 (December 7th 2020 - January 4th 2021) 戊子

Those who have already feeling sickly or late should avoid using this room, as frail health threatens to plague this month. Medical researchers are likely to make successful breakthroughs in their work and medical practitioners will find their advice and services highly sought-after. Those involved in real estate or property are likely to make some handsome gains from their investment in land.

農曆十二月 (January 5th - February 2nd 2021) 己丑

Those of you who are in relationships should put in more effort this month, as romance issues may come to the forefront. Be sure not to take your partner for granted. If you are working in the research and development field, your abilities are most likely to be noticed this month, especially if you are dealing with companies and associates abroad.

Main Door	West	Bedroom Sector	Southeast

農曆正月 (February 4th - March 4th) 戊寅

Instead of trying to look for a long term romantic relationship, you should concentrate on our career and work. Chances are, it is not a month to embark on any romantic relationship. The advantages are that you will be able to indulge yourself wholeheartedly into your career without worrying about how your personal life is going to play out.

農曆二月 (March 5th - April 3rd) 己卯

Business owner are most likely to find your employees to act a little difficult and stubborn than usual. You may have some particularly rocky instances where outright rebellion leads to wasted time and lower productivity. This won't necessarily affect your financial profit if you pay your card right, but be sure to get your hands dirty in terms of finding a solution.

農曆三月 (April 4th - May 4th) 庚辰

It is advisable to focus on your career, as this is not an ideal month to chase after love. Be mindful of rivals launching a hostile takeover bid for your business and be sure to have plans on how to ward the off, just in case. Likewise, employees need to be careful on how to handle workplace conflicts, if they wish to keep their job at the current company.

農曆四月 (May 5th - June 4th) 辛巳

Employees will find their capabilities being recognized by their superior, who may entrust you with more complex projects or assignments. So prove your worth, and that promotion may be just in your bag. The energies in this room are beneficial to romantic relationships, so take the chance to enhance a closer tie with your partners. Likewise, athletes should make an extra effort as this month will support their endeavours.

Main Door	West	Bedroom Sector	Southeast

農曆五月 (June 5th - July 5th) 壬午

It would be a good idea to move the teenagers and youngsters to another room, as they may seem to behave more rebelliously this month. It is advisable to pay extra attention to elderly folks' health. Be sure to seek immediate medical attention for any health issues arising to avoid minor diseases festering into something more serious.

農曆六月 (July 6th - August 6th) 癸未

Refrain from having any negative forms outside of this room, as health problems may be rendered for elderly family members, particularly kidney and stomach ailments. Couples using this room will probably enjoy harmonious time wait each other, and their loved ones. Meanwhile, if you've any real estate investment portfolios under your name, now's a good time to divest of some of them and cash-in on your profits.

農曆七月 (August 7th - September 6th) 甲申

Those who are going to sit for important examinations should tap into the energies of this room, as it is likely to see positive outcomes. Bankers will find their efforts and capabilities being recognized by their superiors, which could lead to a promotion. Likewise, entrepreneurs and budding business owners are likely to see a good start in their ventures.

農曆八月 (September 7th - October 7th) 乙酉

Couples using this room are likely to enjoy a harmonious relationship, as well as excel in their respective career fields. Refrain from making any significant decision, as far as commercial deals are concerned. It is better to bide your time, in waiting for a better moment to make you move. If it is a must to make any deals, be sure only to stick with conservative business deals.

農曆九月 (October 8th - November 6th) 丙戌

Mental and emotional issues may upset you, leave you feeling lonely and isolated from the rest of the world. Be sure to seek company from your loved ones and friend, to bolster your spirits. This would be a great month to tie the knot for the couples and embark upon this latest phase of lives. Likewise, employees who have worked hard the past six month are likely to see rewards coming to them this month.

農曆十月 (November 7th - December 6th) 丁亥

This would be a month full of intense competition and rivalry, especially at the workplace. Be sure to maintain a low profile and always keep your guard up. Remember to keep your cool, to prevent any issues from escalating into something more serious. Where possible, don't burn any bridges because you'll never know when you might need those connections.

農曆十一月 (December 7th 2020 - January 4th 2021) 戊子

The energies in the room is favourable for both professional and personal relationship. Take this opportunity to foster even closer tie with your business partners, colleagues and loved ones. However, be mindful that your employees might be a little more rebellious this month, and your superiors are equally hard to please. Don't let this stand in your way of making a financial gain, although a more hands-on approach will suit you best!

農曆十二月 (January 5th - February 2nd 2021) 己丑

In general, most of you will be able to take on your rivals this month with renewed zeal and energy. Be bold to go full steam ahead, as you are likely to attract new customers by doing so. Word of mouth could result in financial gain for you, especially those in the property industry. So keep your ears to the ground and take necessary steps to cultivate your network of contacts. Teenagers using this room are likely to experience a whirlwind of emotions and feelings. Be mindful not to plunge into anything head-first to avoid having regrets later on.

Main Door	West	Bedroom Sector	East

SE	S	SW
6	2	4
5	**7**	9
1	3	8
NE	N	NW

E — W

農曆正月 **(February 4th - March 4th)** 戊寅

Refrain from making any speculative investments this month, as it could cause you to lose more than you gain. Financial loses often come with extra tension and some emotional imbalance that might lead you to feel depressed. Be sure to talk to a trusted friend or professional if you are experiencing emotionally unstable.

農曆二月 **(March 5th - April 3rd)** 己卯

Any joint-venture projects or businesses should be avoided this month, as the outcomes are likely to be undesirable. Those of you working in the computer industry will find that your rewards don't pay off equally with the amount of blood, sweat, and tears you feel that you have been putting in. Relationships will need your consideration in seeking out solutions that benefit all involved.

農曆三月 **(April 4th - May 4th)** 庚辰

The user of this room should watch out for liver problems this month. Be sure to visit your doctor if you are feeling unwell. It is a good time to cash-in your gains for those who had profited from your investments. However, it is advisable not to put your money in the share market, in case you end up broke at the end of the day. Money should be brought in instead of gambled out this month.

農曆四月 **(May 5th - June 4th)** 辛巳

Children using this room are tending to be more rebellious this month, so be sure to employ tact and patience in handling them. The risk of car accidents is very likely, so be extra cautious whenever you are on the road. This would be a favourable month for the lawyers and mediators.

Main Door	West	Bedroom Sector	East

農曆五月 (June 5th - July 5th) 壬午

All major decision-making shall be postponed to a better time, as rushing into it could only bring negative incomes. Watch out for acts of betrayal within your workplace, and be sure to remain alert of any such potential threads. A family-run business may also be vulnerable to disputes and arguments among family members, and things may get out of hand very quickly if left unchecked.

農曆六月 (July 6th - August 6th) 癸未

Be sure to stay away from unhealthy activities such as smoking and drinking, as these will have negative consequences on your health in the long run. Nevertheless, watch out for kidney problems, particularly kidney stones, as it could plague those using this room this month. CEOs and those in managerial positions are likely to find their wisdom and intelligence bringing about positive outcomes for the company, and as a result, you may have just earned yourself a promotion.

農曆七月 (August 7th - September 6th) 甲申

Those who already feel unwell should avoid this room, as stroke or internal bleeding poses a serious threat. Romantic relationship seems to be more strained and tense, so give each other some breathing space and don't sweat over small issues. However, thanks to the network of contacts and recommendations from satisfied, existing clients, the IT professionals are most likely to do well this month.

農曆八月 (September 7th - October 7th) 乙酉

Couples using this room need to be a little more patient in dealing with their loved ones, as the energies in this room are probably going to leave negative effects on your relationship. Expectant mothers should be extra cautious when using this room. Although there will be money to be made from conservative property-related deals, those in business may find that they are lacking the leverage to benefit from their positive investment outcomes.

農曆九月 (October 8th - November 6th) 丙戌

This could be a rather challenging month for lawyers and legal practitioners, as they will find that it is hard to put their cases across. Watch out for health issues, involving mouth and speech-related problems. Be sure to exercise patience and tolerance in dealing with your partner and spouse, as arguments and tension will only cause discord to your relationship.

農曆十月 (November 7th - December 6th) 丁亥

It is advisable for those who are prone to, or already suffering from depression not to use this bedroom for this month, as the energies present in the room will only exacerbate your situation. Seek company from your friends or loved ones if you are feeling lonely. Bear in mind, it is only a temporary situation, which should soon pass.

農曆十一月 (December 7th 2020 - January 4th 2021) 戊子

Refrain from engaging in any joint-venture this month, as it will most likely to end up in disasters. Always look for a mutually amicable solution to your problems, especially as your relationship is concerned. It is better to practice tolerance and patience to your partners, instead of winning the battle but lose the war. Professionals in the IT industry will see the outcome doesn't equal to the hard work they had been putting in.

農曆十二月 (January 5th - February 2nd 2021) 己丑

Increase profit may be seen for senior personnel in the communication industry. It is advisable to put the bravado aside and consider the situation using reason, as this is a month of physical aggression for males, where jealousy and rivalry among them could result in fights. These could likely end up in the law court. Bear in mind not to put all your expectations into one basket, as this is a month for short-term flings instead of long term relationships.

| Main Door | West | Bedroom Sector | Northeast |

農曆正月 (February 4th - March 4th) 戊寅

Investing in property will be a good idea this month. You are likely to find numerous and handsome profits by selling off property. Likewise, the future outcome for investments made this month is mostly favourable. Expectant mothers should avoid using this room at all costs, as chances for complications and miscarriage are quite high.

農曆二月 (March 5th - April 3rd) 己卯

Elderly folks using this room should pay more attention to health issues, particularly kidney problems. Be sure to check out any signs of illness at its earliest stage. It seems like attention is coming your way this month for the rest of you, especially in the professional sense. Be sure to take this opportunity to get your name out there and make the effort to embark on new alliances and connections.

農曆三月 (April 4th - May 4th) 庚辰

This is a good month to show off your true talent and capabilities to your superior, so be bold to go full steam ahead. Possible promotion or career advancement may be awaiting when you get duly noticed and recognized. If you're in the midst of business negotiation or concluding a deal, you may find the process to be smooth sailing and in your favour.

農曆四月 (May 5th - June 4th) 辛巳

This room bodes well for those who are single and looking to embark on a romantic relationship this month. Be sure to turn on that charm and go all out in ensnaring a potential romantic mate. A surfeit of opportunities will benefit those in the construction industry and literary field. There will be a chance for you to enjoy a good agreement and be able to seal the deal in terms of investment opportunities.

| Main Door | West | Bedroom Sector | Northeast |

農曆五月 (June 5th - July 5th) 壬午

It is advisable to mind your own business and avoid poking your nose into other people's affairs, as you may trigger anger – which could lead to arguments and disputes to be directed at you. Generally, this month will see improvement in your ties with friends and family members, as long as you keep your distance from other people's affairs.

農曆六月 (July 6th - August 6th) 癸未

Relationship will seem to improve for couples after going through some strained complications this month. Things are likely to go back to normal and tie will once again be friendly. Likewise, it will be a good idea to tap into the energies of this room if you are ensnared in a divorce or corporate break-up, as it could lend an air of agreeableness to the proceedings.

農曆七月 (August 7th - September 6th) 甲申

Couples using this room should be wary of the occurrence of suspicion and jealousy. Be sure to make an effort to communicate with each other to dissolve any possible threats. Pregnancy complications including miscarriage are possible this month, so it is best for pregnant ladies to avoid this room at all cost.

農曆八月 (September 7th - October 7th) 乙酉

This room bodes well with those due to sit for important examinations, as the energies here are very conducive to revision and study. A sense of concentration and focus are likely to be heightened, result in better academic performance. In general, the positive vibes in the room are beneficial to academics and scholars.

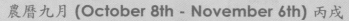

農曆九月 (October 8th - November 6th) 丙戌

Couples are seen to go through a bumpy relationship this month, as quarrels and disagreements are likely to plague their daily lives. Be sure to practice endurance and do not give in to your impulse to say cutting words, which could lead to greater troubles. Do not take your partner for granted and most importantly, try your best to understand what your partner is going through instead of focusing on your personal point of view. Those in the publishing and furniture industries will find this a favourable month, in which many good business opportunities are available.

農曆十月 (November 7th - December 6th) 丁亥

It will probably be a smooth sailing month for those involved in the real estate and property industry, as great progress and developments are in sight. It's time to further enhance your career prospect. It is advisable for the expectant mothers not to use this room, or it could otherwise lead to unnecessary complications.

農曆十一月 (December 7th 2020 - January 4th 2021) 戊子

You will find the spotlight trained on you this month, which will bring you a lot of positive publicity and recognition. Be sure to channel the attention to aid yourself, your career or your business However, the elderly folks should be wary of potential kidney problems. Those in the travel, tourism, or even courier and logistics industries will see positive benefits this month as a result of using the room.

農曆十二月 (January 5th - February 2nd 2021) 己丑

For those in the medical industry will find that your skills are greatly sought-after this month, so handsome profit will be in sight in no time. Investment in property is most likely to see a quick and profitable return. Be sure to consult the experts for guidance whenever you are feeling unsure. Pregnant ladies should avoid using this room at all costs, as chances of miscarriage and other complications are possible.

| Main Door | West | Bedroom Sector | North |

農曆正月 (February 4th - March 4th) 戊寅

Be sure to pay extra attention to your partner, as there may be other parties vying for his/her affections. Be wary about the warning sign, and do not take your partner for granted no matter what. A relationship is like a garden – it needs to be watered and tended to daily.

農曆二月 (March 5th - April 3rd) 己卯

Driving accidents are possible for those using this room this month, so be sure to take extra caution when you get behind the wheel. Make sure you don't drive while intoxicated or fatigued and sleepy. There will be potential problems at work, so be wary of any warning signs to avoid it turning into something much bigger and serious.

農曆三月 (April 4th - May 4th) 庚辰

Speculative investments, especially in the future market, will see handsome profits this month. However, be sure to scrutinize all business deals and contracts carefully, as oversights may cost you a fortune. Relationship may somewhat be strained this month, but the condition can be dissolved through mutual respect. Make sure you discuss with him or her before making any decisions, regardless of minor or major.

農曆四月 (May 5th - June 4th) 辛巳

The energies in the room this month augur well for new business ventures or career changing. For those who are interested in such endeavours, this is the time to embark on your plan. However, public relations specialist may find this a rather challenging month, as unexpected problems seem to crop up from all directions. Bear in mind, be patient and plan carefully. Take good care of your health, particularly your liver.

Main Door	West	Bedroom Sector	North

農曆五月 (June 5th - July 5th) 壬午

It is advisable to mind your own business this month, instead of poking your nose into the affairs of others. Although you can make money and the wisdom to safeguard it, be wary of fraudsters around you in wait to cheat you out of your wealth. Good academic outcomes will also be seen for students who used this room to prepare for their examinations.

農曆六月 (July 6th - August 6th) 癸未

Enjoy your path to success this month by all mean, but be sure watch out for any jealous rivals. For those in the metal and equities markets, your experience and expertise will be recognized and it is a good time to utilize it to your advantages. Beware of health problems in terms of gastrointestinal ailments and limb injuries.

農曆七月 (August 7th - September 6th) 甲申

It's a particularly turbulent month. Friends may find themselves got caught in quarrels over a power-struggle this month, which could lead to the end of friendships, or worse, a possible court case. Make sure that all security procedures are in place, as your employees or even family members may defraud or steal from you.

農曆八月 (September 7th - October 7th) 乙酉

Those using this room may feel stressed and lonely this month. It is advisable to move out of the room for the time being. At the same time, subordinates will see to be a little more rebellious and may be inclined to challenge their superiors and fathers. Elderly males should take care of their health and go for a full medical check-up, to eliminate the risk of suffering from an internal injury or bleeding.

農曆九月 (October 8th - November 6th) 丙戌

Refrain from making any speculative investment or gambling, as it is not a suitable time for such endeavour. Couples need to make sure to communicate with each other more coherently and tactfully, as well as, listen to each other. Unfortunately, those using this room won't exactly be privileged to enjoy robust health, especially males, who will be particularly prone to liver problems.

農曆十月 (November 7th - December 6th) 丁亥

Business owners need to be mindful of the doings of your rivals and competitors, which could undermine your effort. Make sure that you keep your guard up, to eliminate any underhand tactics employed by your rivals. Romantic relationship is very likely to be fraught with mistrust this month as well.

農曆十一月 (December 7th 2020 - January 4th 2021) 戊子

It is advisable to take extra caution when you are behind the wheel, as risks of car accidents are possible this month. Likewise, make sure all your security procedures are in place as well, as the risk of robbery is likely. Be mindful of any problematic situation at the workplace, which could develop into serious scenario if left unchecked.

農曆十二月 (January 5th - February 2nd 2021) 己丑

As financial losses are looming on the horizon, it is best to refrain from any gambling activities. Investments in property or real estate should also be withdrawn before they endure any significant losses. Health problems may raise its head to the ladies using this room this month. Be sure to schedule a full body checkup and mammogram to eliminate possibilities of breast cancer.

| Main Door | West | Bedroom Sector | Northwest |

農曆正月 (February 4th - March 4th) 戊寅

You will likely receive recognition from your superiors, which could lead to a job promotion or salary increment. All your hard work from the previous month will eventually be noticed and appreciated by others. This is also an ideal month to tie the knot for couples who have long thought of marriage.

農曆二月 (March 5th - April 3rd) 己卯

This is generally a good month for working on your professional and personal relationships. Although things may not go smooth at the beginning, they will often work out well in the long run. So don't be afraid to push for some good opportunities, particularly in terms of professional networking. Opportunities to make money are somewhat fleeting this month; nothing worthwhile particularly sticks.

農曆三月 (April 4th - May 4th) 庚辰

Children using this room will see good outcomes for their academic pursuits. Relationships are generally on the upswing, but don't be discouraged if they don't turn out to match your expectations. Those rely on persuasive power to make a living, like the negotiators, should tap into the energies of this room, as it could enhance your capabilities to influence the others with your point of view when concluding important business deals.

農曆四月 (May 5th - June 4th) 辛巳

You will probably see projects progress smoothly this month, with employees being accorded due credit for their respective contributions. Those working in the banking or finance industry are likely to be rewarded with promotion or salary increment this month. Don't hesitate to venture abroad to conclude that deal you've been negotiating over the previous months or years, as the time is right and your persistence will finally pay off.

| Main Door | West | Bedroom Sector | Northwest |

農曆五月 (June 5th - July 5th) 壬午

It is advisable not to focus on looking for love but to focus on your career instead. You might find unexpected rewards from your career. Be extra careful if you are partaking in any extreme or dangerous sports, as risks of injuries are high. You may find multiple property deals choices available for you to consider, but make sure that you know what you want. Think twice before you sign on that dotted line.

農曆六月 (July 6th - August 6th) 癸未

Any overseas business opportunities are likely to yield positive outcomes for you, so be bold to take on any pursuits abroad. This will be a productive month for textile manufacturers and those involved in the fashion industry, with increased profit as a reward at the end of the day. Remember to keep an eye on your employees this month, as dishonest or disloyal staff may well prove to be your bane if left unmonitored.

農曆七月 (August 7th - September 6th) 甲申

Refrain from making important business decisions this month, as they are unlikely to work in your favour and might just cause you to suffer great financial loss. In spite of what appears to be a challenging month, you'll be relieved and pleased to find that the changes will bring about positive consequences. This room also bodes well for adults who want to focus on academic endeavours, or engage in self-cultivation activities.

農曆八月 (September 7th - October 7th) 乙酉

The presence of any water feature in this room augurs well for property-related endeavours and investments. If you are already in a position of authority or high social status, be sure to take advantage of any opportunities headed your way. Health issues of the elderly ladies at home should be taken care of. Be sure to seek immediate medical attention at the first sign of ailments, especially at the stomach area, to prevent them from developing into serious issues.

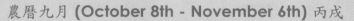

農曆九月 (October 8th - November 6th) 丙戌

Married coupled using this room will find this a harmonious and blissful month for their marital relationship. Those in the construction and engineering business will see their business prosper this month, along with opportunities to invest abroad. Likewise, those who have invested their money into viable portfolios will find their investment rewarding, especially fund managers.

農曆十月 (November 7th - December 6th) 丁亥

This is a favourable month for romantic endeavours and long-term relationships. So, if you are thinking about proposing, this is the time! Couples who are trying to conceive are likely to receive good news and celebrations. Those who have been working hard throughout the past few months, rewards and recognition are headed your way this month.

農曆十一月 (December 7th 2020 - January 4th 2021) 戊子

This is a good time for you to engage in speculative investments in the real estate and property sector, provided that you are in for calculated risks. However, even though you will see plenty of opportunities to make money, you won't be able to capitalise on most of them. Relationships may seem to be a little bumpy at the beginning, but you may want to take advantage of this month to clear any misunderstandings.

農曆十二月 (January 5th - February 2nd 2021) 己丑

The energies of this month augur well for self-cultivation activities. You will see a fruitful result and obtain great satisfaction. So make this your month of self-improvement and consider kick-starting a new regime, or participate in meditation and spiritual activities. It's time to make that important decision that you have been putting on hold, as you will find clarity of thought this month. Overall, health is in good condition, as long as there are no negative features located outside of this room.

Southwest Sector
Main Door

| Main Door | Southwest | Bedroom Sector | Southwest |

This section contains the monthly outlook for all 12 months of the year, for different bedroom sectors in a property with a Southwest Main Door.

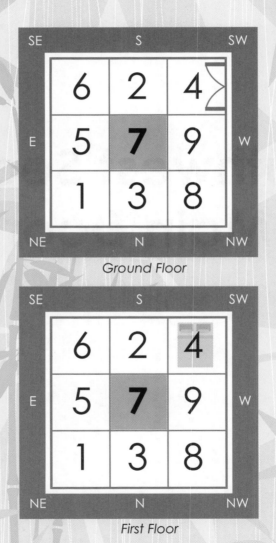

Ground Floor

First Floor

農曆正月 (February 4th - March 4th) 戊寅

Entrepreneurs and businessmen will likely find their employees going the extra mile to produce what is needed as a result of their loyalty. The forestry and dairy farming business will also see growing demands for their products this month. Couples may experience some issues in their relationship, but fret not! Try taking short trips, and give some space to each other, you may find things going well eventually.

農曆二月 (March 5th - April 3rd) 己卯

Female politicians should make use of this time to conclude contracts with their employees, as the contracts will appear to be significant and highly beneficial. Marital tensions are in sight this month, with women being more argumentative than usual. Be sure to check all the electrical wiring in your home, as risks of potential fire hazard are high this month.

農曆三月 (April 4th - May 4th) 庚辰

Those in the real estate or property industry may find businesses to be a bit slow this month, but for those in the fashion, apparel and cosmetics industries, you will see high profit bringing in by business connections this month. Be sure to guard against injuries in your spine, as it could result in more serious complications involving your limbs in the future.

農曆四月 (May 5th - June 4th) 辛巳

The relationship with your in-laws is particularly tense this month. It is best to minimise any form of contact to prevent conflicts from taking place. That aside, this is a fairly favourable month for viable properties investment, especially for those in the media, travel, tourism and farming business.

| Main Door | Southwest | Bedroom Sector | Southwest |

農曆五月 (June 5th - July 5th) 壬午

Couples using this room will enjoy happiness and growth in their relationship this month. Be sure to make use of the energies in the room to develop a closer tie with your partner. It is advisable for pregnant ladies to use another room to prevent pregnancy complications. If you have a long-awaited trip or holiday to go for, this is the time to do so, as the energies this month bode well for such endeavours.

農曆六月 (July 6th - August 6th) 癸未

Be sure to stay away from office politics, especially those in the food and beverage industry, as unfriendly rivalry could escalate out of control and bring serious consequences. Married couples will need to exercise tolerance and patience for each other, as strained relationships are in sight this month. Domestic dispute and family matters may occur this month, and it is more likely to affect the females using this room more than the males.

農曆七月 (August 7th - September 6th) 甲申

The energies in this room bode well with self-development endeavours this month. Those taking self-help course and those attending seminars or workshops should tap into the energies of this room for a better result. Be careful of the females at your workplace, as they could cause trouble at work this month. For those who will be traveling this month, be sure that your travel insurance is in place to prevent any possible problems or issues during your trip.

農曆八月 (September 7th - October 7th) 乙酉

Those using this room will see strong academic luck this month. Students taking important examinations should use this room to their advantage. Those in the literary field should look for publishers this month as the energies of this room augur such endeavours. This is the time to build alliance partners abroad or embark on business expansion, as the outcome is most likely favourable.

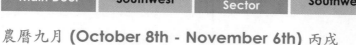
農曆九月 (October 8th - November 6th) 丙戌

Athletes and journalists will enjoy a fairly positive month of output ability, as well as enhancement of your reputation through your work. Likewise, those in the financial industry and literary field will also find their reputation and fame enhanced through finalising deals abroad. Avoid having any negative features outside of this room, as there will be risks of ailments in the kidney or lung area.

農曆十月 (November 7th - December 6th) 丁亥

Financial losses are possible this month, so it is best to refrain from all forms of gambling and speculative activities. It is better to leave all risk-taking decisions related to money to a better time in the future. Certainly, investment in property deals should also be postponed. Women using this room should also pay attention to their health. Ladies should consult your doctor for a full check-up, especially to identify if there are any gynaecological problems. It is best to get it sorted out early.

農曆十一月 (December 7th 2020 - January 4th 2021) 戊子

Relationships will bloom and thrive for couples who use this room, especially the newlyweds. Students who are sitting for important examinations will also benefit from the energies of this room and get favourable results in the examinations. Make sure the necessary insurance policies are in place before you embark on any form of travel, as carelessness is likely.

農曆十二月 (January 5th - February 2nd 2021) 己丑

All investment deals should be avoided, as wealth luck is not in your favour this month. This is also not the month to lend money to others unless you are not expecting to get your money back. Long story short, always be careful when dealing with money-related matters this month. It is advisable to be extra cautious with your daily undertaking, as physical injuries are possible, especially in the head or the bones. It is best to visit the doctor at the first chance possible when minor ailments appear.

Main Door	Southwest	Bedroom Sector	South

SE	S	SW
6	2	4
E 5	**7**	9 **W**
1	3	8
NE	N	NW

農曆正月 (February 4th - March 4th) 戊寅

Employees will probably find it hard to make money this month no matter how hard they work. Finance-wise, losses are possible this month, so be sure any deals done this month will not rely on any capital. However, those in the legal field are likely to find increased demand for their skills by their clients and potential new customers.

農曆二月 (March 5th - April 3rd) 己卯

Refrain from getting involved in the financial markets this month, as the chances of sustaining heavy losses are high. Ladies using this room should be wary of illness and accidents, consult a doctor at the first sign of unwell, to prevent ailments from developing into serious complications. This will prove to be a difficult month for those in merchant banking, shares, stocks, and equities, as deals go belly-up in many cases and profits start to dwindle.

農曆三月 (April 4th - May 4th) 庚辰

Expectant mothers should be careful when using this room, as pregnancy complications are likely this month. Be sure to see your doctor if anything is feeling not right. The energies in the room are likely to cause unnecessary disharmony and disputes between couples who stay in the room. So it is best to move out of it temporarily.

農曆四月 (May 5th - June 4th) 辛巳

Couples using this room are probably going to spend the month quarrelling and arguing. Make sure all your traffic fines and outstanding taxes are cleared to avoid catching by the long arms of the law. Those working in the property development business should work aggressively to enjoy the fruit of labour from your hard work.

農曆五月 (June 5th - July 5th) 壬午

Refrain from having any negative Sha outside of this room, especially if you have pregnant ladies at home, as risks of miscarriage are possible. If you noticed any water outside of this room, all property deals should take a backseat to avoid heavy losses. There is a chance of windfall gains this month – and this is especially true for the older women of the family.

農曆六月 (July 6th - August 6th) 癸未

This room don't bode well for endeavours that involves deep thinking and critical analysis. Therefore, it is preferable not to make any important decision at this point, as confusion will come into the decision-making process for those using this room this month. Students should avoid using this room as well if they are due to sit for examinations this month.

農曆七月 (August 7th - September 6th) 甲申

It is advisable to postpone all important decision-making, as otherwise, this could result in less desirable decisions being made that may cause some regret later. Women of the house tend to be stubborner and foolish this month. It would be better not to take any new relationship seriously this month, as they may not be what they seem and may start to lose their initial lustre after some time.

農曆八月 (September 7th - October 7th) 乙酉

Those in the real estate and property development will find this a favourable month to make beneficial investments in property this month. If you are expecting a promotion to the position of authority and high social status, this might be the time you are getting what you always wanted. Be mindful of heart and eye problems for those who are using this room.

農曆九月 (October 8th - November 6th) 丙戌

Judges and doctors will find their service and advice in great demand this month, especially if times are particularly difficult. Be sure to avoid this room if you wish to start a family, as the energies of this bedroom will not be conducive. Health-wise, be mindful of burns and scalding by hot water.

農曆十月 (November 7th - December 6th) 丁亥

Ensure that you had settled all outstanding traffic fines, summonses and taxes to avoid catching up by the long arm of the law. The energies of this room this month tend to bring about disagreements, misunderstandings, and disputes. Couples using this bedroom are likely to find themselves quarrelling with each other more frequently than usual this month. It is advisable to exercise tolerance and patience to your partner at this critical moment.

農曆十一月 (December 7th 2020 - January 4th 2021) 戊子

This is probably the best time to invest in real estate, as handsome profits will return in the form of a quick buck. Medical practitioners will find increased demand for their skills and there will be plenty of opportunities to serve the sick and needy. Males who are going through divorce proceedings will find matters going difficult as their partners gain more leverage over them for benefits and assets.

農曆十二月 (January 5th - February 2nd 2021) 己丑

Those who are already prone to emotional instability should be careful when using this room. Emotional and psychological issues are likely to plague those staying in this room and cause some discontent. Those working in the marketing and media industry will find this a rather difficult month, as result or gains are unsatisfying despite all your pushing and prodding. It is best to play it safe when striking business deals this month. Go with your gut instinct to trust people you've dealt with before instead of going down a whole new path.

農曆正月 (February 4th - March 4th) 戊寅

Those in the legal field will find strong demand for their skills this month. However, be mindful of unnecessary gossips. The relationship is likely to present in short-term passionate flings. It is better not to put in high expectations in the hope of making it a long-term relationship. Jealousy and rivalry will be intense this month. So, ensure that you keep a low profile, or otherwise it could result in possible legal issues.

農曆二月 (March 5th - April 3rd) 己卯

Loyal employees will find to receive long-awaited rewards from the company this month as a result of your effort throughout this time. Avoid putting too much pressure on your staff. They may perform better when the pressure is off of them. For those involved in professional sport, you are most likely to outshine your rivals in the sports arena.

農曆三月 (April 4th - May 4th) 庚辰

This turns out to be a challenging month for those in the banking, equities, and financial industries, so avoid concluding major deals now, as these will only bring you more headache and stress. Also, beware of betrayal from certain employees. Elderly ladies should avoid using this room this month, as the energies there will only make them more susceptible to lung infection.

農曆四月 (May 5th - June 4th) 辛巳

Couples, especially newlyweds will find this a good month to travel, as they will find and share growth experience in many respects. Those involved in the academic and literary fields will also find good financial gains this month, brought by inspirations and new ideas that come to them along the way. Those making speculative investments in equities and stock will probably hear some good news but be sure to keep a low profile and conceal this windfall.

Main Door	Southwest	Bedroom Sector	Southeast

農曆五月 (June 5th - July 5th) 壬午

Be careful when you are behind the wheel this month, as the likelihood of accidents is high. Parents may want to pay extra attention to their children for they may be more rebellious this month. Employees in the engineering industry will enjoy full support from their superior this month, even with a chance of salary increment!

農曆六月 (July 6th - August 6th) 癸未

Good profits from property deals are likely to come to those in the real estate industry and using this room this month. Generally, this is a beneficial month for the insurance agents, so it's time to venture out and expand your business. Bouts of depression will be creeping in for those using this room this month, so if you are already prone to emotional disturbance, it is better to change a room.

農曆七月 (August 7th - September 6th) 甲申

It is generally a good month for health and relationship. Those in the logistics, courier and tourism industries will see their business prosper as well. If your job involves strategic decision-making or sound analytic skills, it's time to show the world your worth! It is the best opportunity to make a name for yourself, which in turn, further brighten your career prospects.

農曆八月 (September 7th - October 7th) 乙酉

Internal bickering may occur at work this month. It is best to keep a low profile and stay out of all office politics. Avoid taking sides in any arguments. Be sure to remove any negative structure outside of this room, as there will be a high chance of the son may challenge the status and authority of the father. Family discords are likely. Elderly men should watch out for health problems, especially issues related to blood and lung disease.

農曆九月 (October 8th - November 6th) 丙戌

Good news is in sight for investment and merchant bankers who conclude deals in the share and equities market, as profits will occur soon enough for you to enjoy. Indeed, all your hard work and effort will finally be recognized by your superior. You will probably see a promotion or a salary increment this month. However, those using this room will somehow be feeling lonely and emotional.

農曆十月 (November 7th - December 6th) 丁亥

Business partners are likely to find themselves involved in disagreements with each other. There is a high possibility that the elder partner will prevail at the end of the day. Likewise, couples will also find to squabble and bicker endlessly. It is best if you can take some time away from your home and go on a vacation to sort things out. Elderly folks should watch out for ailments affecting their kidney this month.

農曆十一月 (December 7th 2020 - January 4th 2021) 戊子

Jealous rivals and enemies will find chances to undermine you, so be sure to use your wits to counter their devious schemes. Competitive athletes will probably do well in tournaments. Here's a great chance for those who wish to make a name for themselves, as this month bodes well with promotions and career advancements.

農曆十二月 (January 5th - February 2nd 2021) 己丑

This is a favourable month for you in all aspects! You will see good wealth luck, with the opportunity to make financial gain in the real estate and property industries. At the same time, your personal relationship is likely to enjoy pleasantly good vibes. So be sure to spend more time with your loved ones and the people you care about, as this emotional investment will bring about its own rewards. For business owners, it's time to attract new customers and clients and make new connections to earn solid financial returns. It's time to try out new ideas and techniques to experiment on different responses.

農曆正月 (February 4th - March 4th) 戊寅

Be wary of kidney and eye problems this month, as risks are possible. It is advisable to move into another room; as the frosty relationship may occur if you continue using this room. Instead of driving to improve strategic and financial directive, CEOs should spend more time motivating their staff, as otherwise, unmotivated staff will prove to be more of a problem in the coming month.

農曆二月 (March 5th - April 3rd) 己卯

All risky business dealings should be avoided, as losses related to property transactions are possible. There is a tendency of health issues turning to worse conditions this month, so do not take any minor illness lightly. Pregnancy complications are likely in this room, so it is best for the expectant ladies to move into another room where possible.

農曆三月 (April 4th - May 4th) 庚辰

Hygiene problems should be the top of your concern list unless you wish to be plagued by any form of skin disease. It's one thing to overindulge in alcohol, and another altogether to get involved in a casual relationship or one-night stand, as a result! Refrain from any form of traveling this month, as it is probably going to fraught with difficulties and problems causing you stress and exasperation in the process.

農曆四月 (May 5th - June 4th) 辛巳

It is best to avoid ventured and projects which need support from your staff, as this will not be a good month to rely on your employees. They are only going to trigger more trouble than they are worth. If it is necessary to conclude investment deals, it is better to stay with the blue chips for the best chance of returns. Couples will also need to be wary of arguments and disputes.

Main Door	Southwest	Bedroom Sector	East

農曆五月 (June 5th - July 5th) 壬午

Refrain from taking up risky business dealings and property related transactions as financial losses are most profitable. Avoid starting anything new this month, as obstructions are likely and projects may end up in failed ventures. It is best to lie low and recuperate from the previous months. Health is poor this month, so stay away from this room if you are already suffering from gastrointestinal problems.

農曆六月 (July 6th - August 6th) 癸未

Business owners and managers will find this to be a difficult month, as it becomes particularly hard to meet sales target, especially for the tourism, travel and media business. Relationships tends to be strained for couples who use this room. It is advisable to move into another room to prevent exacerbating troubles and cause more stress for both parties. Take extra care of your health this month, especially to bladder and kidney problems.

農曆七月 (August 7th - September 6th) 甲申

Be sure to check the electrical wiring at home and get it replaced at once when necessary, as fire hazards are possible this month. Religious enthusiasm using this room could end up in fanaticism. It is better to delay all investment deals and focus on employee motivation instead. Distraction by monetary issues could result in financial ruin for you from which it'll be hard to extricate yourself.

農曆八月 (September 7th - October 7th) 乙酉

Refrain from making high-risk investment deals, as the outcome could be unfavourable, especially where the property industry is concerned. Be wary of financial and relationship problems, as it could exacerbate emotional and mental instability this month. It is advisable to focus on consolidating business positions instead of doing expansions.

農曆九月 (October 8th - November 6th) 丙戌

Miscommunications and misunderstanding may prove to be the problem for couples this month. So be sure to communicate openly and clearly to prevent ill-feelings. Pay extra attention to health issues, especially throat and mouth cancer. See a doctor if there is any sign of unwell, and check it as soon as possible. Problems will seem hard to resolve this month as the cause is not readily identifiable.

農曆十月 (November 7th - December 6th) 丁亥

The tendency of disloyal among employees and subordinates is possible this month. Watch out for any sign of dissatisfaction and trouble. It is advisable to seek immediate medical treatment if you find yourself to be rather anxious and mentally stressed out. This is not an ideal time to finalize any deals, so it is better to wait for a suitable time to make your move.

農曆十一月 (December 7th 2020 - January 4th 2021) 戊子

Heart ailments and complications are particularly affecting those using this room, so it is best to consult your physician at the first sign of trouble. It is advisable for those in the fashion and beauty industry to maintain a low profile, as it will prove to be a difficult month. No major decisions or investments shall be made this month, as they will most likely to result in financial loss.

農曆十二月 (January 5th - February 2nd 2021) 己丑

Those working in the legal and advertising industries will find an increasing demand for your skill, which would lead to possible financial gain. However, beware of jealousy and competition at the workplace, as it could cause some messy legal issues if left unattended. Those of you in the throes of new love would do well to bear in mind that these are likely to be short-term rather than long-term, so keep your expectations in proportion.

| Main Door | Southwest | Bedroom Sector | Northeast |

農曆正月 (February 4th - March 4th) 戊寅

Business owners will find it difficult to get businesses going this month, so don't worry or push yourself too hard. It is best to lie low at the moment and gather ammunition to launch an improvement in the future. Financial loss is likely this month, so stay clear from speculative investment this month, especially gambling and equity investment.

農曆二月 (March 5th - April 3rd) 己卯

This is a good time to conclude deals abroad, especially if it involved asset acquisition. However, make sure you know when to stop, as otherwise, you will only end up going through monetary loss. Students using this room will find themselves experience great academic luck. Likewise, a romantic relationship is likely to do well in this room as well.

農曆三月 (April 4th - May 4th) 庚辰

Those in the furniture industry will see their business prosper this month. Relationships is rather strained for couples using this room. Be sure to exercise greater tolerance and patience during this time. Watch out for your behaviours, as lawsuits and people talking behind your back could prove expensive this month.

農曆四月 (May 5th - June 4th) 辛巳

Marital tension tends to be the problem of this month for married couples using this room. Learn to be more tolerant of each other and learn to adjust your expectations of each other accordingly. Expectant mothers should refrain from using this room, as chances of miscarriage are high. Likewise, move to another room if you are already feeling unwell, as otherwise, you may be more susceptible to illnesses.

| Main Door | Southwest | Bedroom Sector | Northeast |

農曆五月 (June 5th - July 5th) 壬午

You will find this a good month to showcase your talent and work towards building your reputation. Relationships are good and will go well in regards to work this month, with a high possibility of travel. Utilize your inner talent and knowledge to make inroad at work this month. You will see yourself making a good headway if you are proactive at doing this.

農曆六月 (July 6th - August 6th) 癸未

There will be career advancement opportunities for those working in the transportation industry, and they are probably going to receive the promotion they have been eyeing. People from the entertainment industry should also seek the opportunity to advance your career, as your passion and excitement will get you ready for new challenges. Those in the technical field or hands-on work will find this month bringing in many benefits.

農曆七月 (August 7th - September 6th) 甲申

Those who work with machinery or are involved in professional sports should take advantage of the opportunities at your disposal, and you are likely to see favourable outcome in your daily undertakings. Those involved in the real estate industry will find this a good month for investment opportunities. If you are single and looking to form a relationship, this is the room to use as all prospects are good for developing a romantic relationship.

農曆八月 (September 7th - October 7th) 乙酉

This is an unfavourable month for relationships. Things are likely to end badly and leave bad effects or damages to your reputation. Be prepared to brace open and intense challenges from jealous colleagues and peers this month. It is best to ignore and avoid getting involved, or it is likely to work against you. Be particularly careful when you are on the road, as there is an increased risk of car accidents, especially if you have been drinking or driving when fatigued.

農曆九月 (October 8th - November 6th) 丙戌

Politicians and those in public service will enjoy excellent public support this month, which may lead to rising status or ranks in the government or their respective political parties. Be bold and network more this month, as the energies in the room augur such endeavours. Foreign markets and alliances, or partnerships with business owners in other countries are likely to see handsome profits this month.

農曆十月 (November 7th - December 6th) 丁亥

Refrain from making speculative investments, especially gambling and equity investments this month, as the likelihood of financial loss is high. You may also want to watch out for health issues in the lung and head injuries. Things may seem hard to proceed this month, so it is best for business owners to lie low and consolidating your position at this point instead of making aggressive decisions and moves.

農曆十一月 (December 7th 2020 - January 4th 2021) 戊子

Student may find themselves acquiring strong academic luck using this room this month. Be sure to use this room as a study or bedroom to tap into the energies, in order to see favourable outcome in your academic. This will also be a good room to use to further any serious relationship this month, as long as there is no natural water in this room. All overseas deals shall be concluded this month, especially if it involves asset acquisition.

農曆十二月 (January 5th - February 2nd 2021) 己丑

Couples will find their relationship rather strained this month, so be sure to be more tolerant and forgiving. Remember not to utter cutting words to each other, even though if you are really in the temper, as it could only cause further hardship in your relationship. Those of you who are writers – or wishing to be one! – should get your journals and notebooks out and start scribbling! You will find this month augurs well and are conducive for any literary pursuits. Who knows, you may be the next J.K. Rowling!

農曆正月 (February 4th - March 4th) 戊寅

Watch out for your personal belongings this month, as there is a likelihood of financial loss as a result of theft or fraud this month. Internal injuries will prove to be a problem to those who are already feeling unwell, so if you are already prone to health conditions, refrain from reckless actions and push your body to its limit. Health should be on top of the list of your concerns this month. Speculative investment in the financial instrument is likely to see good results this month.

農曆二月 (March 5th - April 3rd) 己卯

The possibility of recognition, rewards, and advancement is likely in the workplace, and you may have the chance of being promoted to positions of power. This is your time to prove your worth, so be sure to put your best foot forward! Parents may find this a difficult month as their sons may challenge their authority. A change of room may be of benefit to tame and calm their sons' rebellious spirits. Elderly men should watch out for lung problems this month.

農曆三月 (April 4th - May 4th) 庚辰

Refrain from making high-risk investments this month as there could be hidden problems, which could be of a legal nature, in the investments. It is best to avoid such investments or otherwise, you might find yourself in too deep in some legal troubles. Giving each other some breathing space could benefit your marital relationship this month.

農曆四月 (May 5th - June 4th) 辛巳

Business owners should watch out of rival posing as allies and bring damage to the financial status of your enterprise. There could be competitors on the horizon in terms of relationships. Couples should make an effort to work out on their relationship. Be sure to appreciate your partner and do not take them for granted, or you might find others are more than willing to step into your shoes. Those in the literary and creative arts field will find fame and enhanced reputation this month, which could bring an increase in wealth.

Main Door	Southwest	Bedroom Sector	North

農曆五月 (June 5th - July 5th) 壬午

Those in the analytical or scientific field will find breakthroughs in their line of work, as a result of the good energies from this room. Those in the mining and construction businesses will find that they make inroads into their competitors' markets this month. This will be a challenging month for those who are refusing to make required changes in their line of work.

農曆六月 (July 6th - August 6th) 癸未

Those making speculative investments, especially in the futures market, will find favourable profits from their investments this month. Relationships seem to be rather strained this month, so it is best to be more tolerant of each other to avoid arguments and disputes. Be on guard for any possibility of legal issues caused by financial problems this month, as otherwise, you may experience loss of income and those losses will be difficult to recoup.

農曆七月 (August 7th - September 6th) 甲申

Those who wish to change careers or embark on new business should make the move this month. The energies in the room bode well for starting anew or beginning new things. The risk of robbery increased this month, so securities should watch out and scrutinize thoroughly during your duty. Those working in the legal industry will do well this month, however, the money and rewards from your efforts can only be collected later.

農曆八月 (September 7th - October 7th) 乙酉

This proves to be a good room for the children to use, as the energies bode well with academic and educational activities. Clarity of thoughts is at its peak this month, so all strategic decisions should be put into action this month to see positive results forthcoming. Beware of unusually good investment deals that could be scams in disguise, as this will result in financial loss and may lead to legal issues.

農曆九月 (October 8th - November 6th) 丙戌

Refrain from having negative forms in this room to prevent eye problems for those who are staying in this room. Be careful not to allow any eyes troubles develop. It is an excellent month to expand your business if you are in the restaurant business. Business owners who worked hard to float their companies will find this a favourable month, as it will be kind to you in terms of those endeavours!

農曆十月 (November 7th - December 6th) 丁亥

Recognition from the superior will come to the professionals in the engineering and technical industry, which could lead to possible promotion and salary increment. However, as an employer, don't be surprised or disheartened to find your subordinates seemingly working against each other. There is a likelihood of emotional problems for those using this room. There shall be no shame in seeking professional help if you feel you need it or talk to a trusted friend.

農曆十一月 (December 7th 2020 - January 4th 2021) 戊子

You may find yourself somewhat on the wrong track this month, but things can be fixed if you are willing to be flexible and ready to make necessary changes. Anxious may prove to be a problem this month when you encounter problems at work, don't worry too much as things will eventually sort themselves out in time. Those in the scientific, research and analytical industry will find this month to be productive, as their skills are much sought-after by interested parties.

農曆十二月 (January 5th - February 2nd 2021) 己丑

It is best to avoid concluding business deals and ventures this month, as the result is unlikely to be favourable. Any forms of investment should also be avoided, especially in the stock market, as it could only cause financial loss. Strained and tense relationships are likely to be experienced by the couples using this room. Instead of pushing the matter, it is better to give each other some breathing space and things will return to normal.

Main Door	Southwest	Bedroom Sector	Northwest

農曆正月 (February 4th - March 4th) 戊寅

Stagnant careers may receive a boost caused by big changes this month. Be careful of sharp metal objects or dangerous metal implements for the young children staying in this room. It is best to move them into another room to prevent unnecessary injuries. The energies in this room bode well with self-cultivation or academic activities, so those using this room are likely to be benefits in terms of personal growth and maturation.

農曆二月 (March 5th - April 3rd) 己卯

Elderly women using this room should pay more attention to minor stomach ailments and get treatment as early as possible, as these could develop into something more serious. Those in authority or of high social status will find things are in their favour this month so take advantage of any opportunity that comes your way. Profitable property deals shall present themselves to you and be sure that you are ready to take advantage of them as soon as they appear.

農曆三月 (April 4th - May 4th) 庚辰

Those working in the travel or logistics industry will see improved profits this month. Couples using this room will find themselves enjoying a harmonious relationship this month, even so, if they are planning to start a new family, they are likely to receive good news. Be wary of bladder-related ailments, especially for the elderly folks using this room.

農曆四月 (May 5th - June 4th) 辛巳

Recognition will come from something you have succeeded in, and promotion is likely in sight! Those using this room will find this is a month of celebration, good news, and happy activities. Short-term flings and passionate romances await this month, so be prepared to brace some romantic intrigue and keep your life spicy by being open-minded to new developments.

農曆五月 (June 5th - July 5th) 壬午

This month will be beneficial to profitable and long-term deals in real estate and property, as it would produce increased profits. Be sure to grab every possible opportunity with renewed gusto. Personal relationship will require a concentrated effort to keep things stable, as it is likely to come under strain this month. Be wary of rivals at works as they may try to plot your downfall, and things could turn ugly in the end.

農曆六月 (July 6th - August 6th) 癸未

Couples will enjoy a harmonious relationship this month with the previous efforts put in. Although they may be a few arguments to occasionally disrupt the peace but things are eventually going well this month. There will be possible windfall gains, so be sure to realize these profits in your portfolio. However, it is important to manage the money well rather than letting it slip through your fingers. Those using this room should avoid having a negative structure located in this room to prevent risks of lung infections.

農曆七月 (August 7th - September 6th) 甲申

For those working in the banking industry, you can expect an increment for the effort you had been putting in that is finally noticed by your superiors. However, females using this room may experience a certain level of loneliness. Professional sportsperson who show their talents to the world will receive recognition and fame as they draw attention to their abilities.

農曆八月 (September 7th - October 7th) 乙酉

Couples will enjoy harmonious relationship and thriving this month, so it's time to foster closer ties with your business partners, colleagues, and loved ones. Property investment will see substantial gains this month, especially if there is a body of water located outside of this room. Females using this room should be mindful of acquiring any chronic abdominal problems or ailments.

農曆九月 (October 8th - November 6th) 丙戌

Be sure to watch your back to safeguard your own interest. Do not let superior take advantage of you and end up getting benefits at your expense. Those in the management and consulting will do well to expand their businesses this month, as both profits and clients abound. The energies in this room bode well with health improvement, so if you in need of recovery from a health ailment, this is the room you should use this month.

農曆十月 (November 7th - December 6th) 丁亥

Be mindful not to get swayed too easily by any romantic interludes you encounter this month, as it is likely to turn out to be short-term flings. Rewards may be headed to you for your diligent efforts at work, in the form of a promotion and salary increment. Indeed, this month promises to be beneficial in good tidings, celebrations and happy events.

農曆十一月 (December 7th 2020 - January 4th 2021) 戊子

With both diligent and preserving, you will see wealth luck smiles upon you this month and you will be able to enjoy the fruit of your labour at the end of the day. Substantial profits are also likely by investing in long-term real estate or property deals, however, be sure that they are viable and proceed carefully. Be mindful of disputes and arguments with your partner or spouse, deal with any tacky situation swiftly and tactfully, to prevent it from getting out of hand.

農曆十二月 (January 5th - February 2nd 2021) 己丑

Business owners should conduct regular audits to ensure that nothing is going the wrong way, as fraud may cost you a fortune. It is better to be safe than sorry. Profits are likely to be gain with your connections, so it's time to make the most out of them! It is also a good time to gain mass exposure for your business or your work by engaging the mass media, so be sure to plan well and go all out on a well-thought publicity blitz.

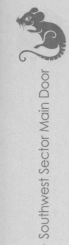

Main Door	Southwest	Bedroom Sector	West

SE	S	SW
6	2	4
5 (E)	**7**	**9** (W)
1	3	8
NE	N	NW

農曆正月 (February 4th - March 4th) 戊寅

Those of you who are involved in speculative property investment and the equities market will find substantial gains coming your way this month. This is also a good month for love for those using this room. However, be sure to evaluate potential partners reasonably and not get too carried away.

農曆二月 (March 5th - April 3rd) 己卯

The energies in this room are conducive enough to allow you to promote and commercialise your ideas, with the aid of the necessary financial backing for your research. So go ahead and apply for that grant you've been eyeing. You will find good outcomes as a result. It's the time to make the most of your opportunities, so do all you can to promote your ideas to the right people.

農曆三月 (April 4th - May 4th) 庚辰

This room bodes well with meditative, spiritual and religious pursuits this month. Travelling will most likely bring about significant rewards, especially if you're in the midst of concluding deals in the precious metal industry. Likewise, new inroads will be paved for those in the media, marketing, and consultancy industry, with possible offers by financial intermediaries to provide the capital needed.

農曆四月 (May 5th - June 4th) 辛巳

Politician and civil servants who have worked hard will find good news and celebrations await. They are likely to receive a promotion to a higher position by virtue of their efforts. If you are in a committed relationship, it is a good time to take your relationship to the next level or formalise it. Financial gains are possible from speculative investments in properties and real estate.

| Main Door | Southwest | Bedroom Sector | West |

農曆五月 (June 5th - July 5th) 壬午

Speculative investment in the metal and equities markets will produce favourable outcomes this month, however, do not get overzealous in pouring in your hard-earned money in high-risk portfolios. Those using this room may expect to be transferred within their organisation where work is concerned, but on more favourable terms and perks due to their hard work. Pay attention to health issues, be sure not to overlook minor ailments.

農曆六月 (July 6th - August 6th) 癸未

Business-related travels are likely to be favourable and profitable for those using this room. So, pack your bag and get ready to make money. Watch out for disgruntled employees and keep your guard up, as their actions will probably lead to troubles. All in all, this promises to be a favourable month, where those using this room stand to reap the fruits of their labour soon enough.

農曆七月 (August 7th - September 6th) 甲申

Don't let work-related stress get the best of you. Be sure to plan your schedule and manage your time better to achieve work-life balance. Refrain from engaging in any speculative investments or gambling, as you will only risk incurring huge financial losses if you do so. Expectant mothers are also advised not to use this room to prevent any complications that could result in a miscarriage.

農曆八月 (September 7th - October 7th) 乙酉

This is a good month to invest in the financial markets, as any viable investments made will tend to be profitable. Students sitting for examinations will find the energies of this room to be beneficial for their endeavours. Couples who wish to seek harmony and romance in their relationship should tap into the positive vibes of this room.

農曆九月 (October 8th - November 6th) 丙戌

Those using this room may need to travel to generate their income this month. Be sure to scrutinise all legal documents before committing yourself to them to eliminate the possibility of any legal complications later on. Couples looking to conceive should use this room for positive results.

農曆十月 (November 7th - December 6th) 丁亥

Romance luck may be in sight for you this month, but be mindful not to overlook the more important virtues of this person underneath his or her outer charm. Also, those using this room should be wary of health issues related to the eyes this month. Considerable gains are likely from speculative property investment and in the equities market.

農曆十一月 (December 7th 2020 - January 4th 2021) 戊子

Personal and professional relationships will see positive progress this month, so take the opportunity to consolidate your ties with the others. There will also be rewards coming to you in the form of recognition and possible promotion for those using this room. But bear in mind, with greater power comes greater responsibility. Be prepared for a more demanding schedule in the upcoming months.

農曆十二月 (January 5th - February 2nd 2021) 己丑

You will find plenty of good deals to be made especially in the real estate business. However, be sure to exercise your analytical ability to choose the right ones and make a home run! It will be worth your time to be completely thorough in checking out credentials. It is particularly important that you vet through all the information you come across this month. Elderly males using this room will do well to get their health problems checked out early this month.

South Sector
Main Door

Main Door	South	Bedroom Sector	South

This section contains the monthly outlook for all 12 months of the year, for different bedroom sectors, in a property with a South Main Door.

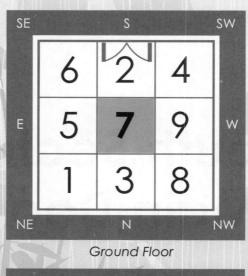

Ground Floor

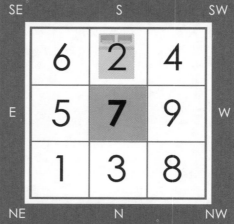

First Floor

農曆正月 (February 4th - March 4th) 戊寅

There is a likelihood of being affected by mental and emotional strain, which may cause stress or even hallucination for you. Be wary not to let stress get to you too much, or else your mental health will suffer. Be sure not to conclude any deals relying on the capital this month, as this may end in serious financial loss. Employees may find it difficult to make money, no matter how hard they work.

農曆二月 (March 5th - April 3rd) 己卯

There will be a chance of superior property deals this month if you are well-prepared with your homework, but remember to tie up all loose ends as neglect them may lead to legal issues later. Try to avoid using this room, as there is a likelihood of serious illness this month. Be sure to scrutinise all details and exercise extreme caution when dealing with legal documents. Make sure you double-check everything before you sign.

農曆三月 (April 4th - May 4th) 庚辰

It is best to delay any decisions to invest in real estate, at least, until the month is over. You may need to expand your energy and time on mediating any discord on the domestic front, such as misunderstandings that entangled relatives and family members in disputes. Expectant mothers should avoid using this room, as there is a very high possibility of miscarriage or premature for pregnant ladies.

農曆四月 (May 5th - June 4th) 辛巳

Any dealings related to real estate or properties may result in financial loss, as it is not an ideal time to invest in real estate. Watch out for potential eye affliction this month. It is best to consult your physician at the first sign of unwell. On the domestic front, you may find the elder ladies at home behaving in a more adamant and possibly, foolhardy manner than usual. It's time to be more patient and try to understand their viewpoint and disgruntlement by sitting down and talking to them where possible.

Main Door	South	Bedroom Sector	South

農曆五月 (June 5th - July 5th) 壬午

Be mindful of your health this month if you are already suffering from a chronic illness of any sort. It is very likely for the risk of your ailment rearing its ugly head again, so it is better to adopt a healthy lifestyle and consult your doctor at the first sign of trouble. Refrain from having any negative features in this room, as these could indicate troubles involving older women. However, the good news is that property or real estate dealings are most likely to land you substantial financial gains.

農曆六月 (July 6th - August 6th) 癸未

Be sure to get your wiring and electrical apparatus checked in your home or office, more so if you notice the presence of any negative feature outside this room. Watch out for the interactions between the women in your household or among your staff, as the probability of misunderstandings and discord is very likely among members of the fairer sex this month. Couples who wished to start a family should avoid this room, as the energies present will only be undermining your objective by doing so.

農曆七月 (August 7th - September 6th) 甲申

This is especially for those who are religious, superstitious or simply believe in the paranormal or supernatural: Avoid using this room this month to prevent any unwanted 'interludes' of the supernatural kind. Refrain from having any negative structures or features outside this room, or else you may find your money being siphoned away from you. However, the good news is that, if you follow these advisories, this will be a relatively comfortable and smooth-sailing month for you.

農曆八月 (September 7th - October 7th) 乙酉

It is advisable to resist temptations to engage in any high-risk ventures this month, as you may end up even poorer at the end of the day. It is obviously not the time to commit to any major or significant deals. Those using this room, especially elderly women, should be mindful of any abdominal ailments this month, and be sure to seek immediate medical treatment at the first sign of trouble.

農曆九月 (October 8th - November 6th) 丙戌

Beware of injuries resulting from sharp metal objects or any metal-based implements, especially for older women of the household. If you noticed the presence of negative Sha in the room, you may also want to be mindful of a potential risk of fire hazard. The energies this room bode well with, especially those involved in athletics or competitive sport, and may lead to a positive outcome if these people tap into the energies of the room.

農曆十月 (November 7th - December 6th) 丁亥

Refrain from having negative features outside this room or legal entanglements may rear their ugly heads just when you least expect them. The more possible outcomes include speeding summons, or even worse, complicated lawsuits. It is better to move your children into another room, as they may become more argumentative and difficult to handle this month. It seems that the energies in this room are the harbinger of trouble this month as relationships are concerned because even disputes and petty bickering involving elderly women are among the outcome for those using this room this month.

農曆十一月 (December 7th 2020 - January 4th 2021) 戊子

There is a high possibility of obtaining substantial financial gains by investing in real estate or property but be sure to vet through every detail and deals carefully before committing yourself to it. If you notice the presence of a significant body of water outside of this room, it is better to call off any property deals, as this is a likely indicator of impending heavy losses. Ladies using this room will tend to behave in a more domineering and assertive manner. Also, they should take care of their health, as they are particularly susceptible to stomach-related ailments.

農曆十二月 (January 5th - February 2nd 2021) 己丑

Those working in the media and marketing industry are probably going to enjoy their fruit of labour this month, which brings great achievements and high honour. Don't worry too much and try to enjoy what comes your way. It is best to move away from this room, especially for those who suffered from depression and related issues. Beware of covert, underhanded schemes by your rivals will only lead to financial loss, and possible legal problems through fraud or embezzlement.

Main Door	South	Bedroom Sector	Southeast

農曆正月 (February 4th - March 4th) 戊寅

Lawyers and professionals working in the legal field will find their skills and service very much sought-after this month. However, you should watch out for disputes and office politics in the form of power struggles. Remember not to give your heart away too easily because chances are, any romantic fling will remain what it is. So don't put high hope in it or expect anything long-term to develop out of it.

農曆二月 (March 5th - April 3rd) 己卯

There will be money to be made from your travels, so pack your suitcase and get ready to hit the road! Employees, especially those working in the media and travel line, will also find their career prosper to a higher position this month with a possible salary increment. Sportspersons and athletes will also excel in competition and tournaments this month!

農曆三月 (April 4th - May 4th) 庚辰

This is a good month to conclude deals in the share and equity markets for the investment and merchant bankers, as it is likely to gain good profits from the deals. Therefore, be sure to grab every possible opportunity. You are probably going to receive recognition, career advancement and financial reward this month, promoting your career to new heights and bring about a whole new level of job satisfaction. Newly-weds will get to enjoy a harmonious relationship this month, as a result of better communication and improved ties.

農曆四月 (May 5th - June 4th) 辛巳

It is best to stay away from trivial disputes or arguments in the workplace, for it could fester into legal complications if blown out of proportion. Just concentrate on your job and all shall be good for you. This is a good month to foster closer ties in both your personal and professional relationships. So it's time to expand your energy on a more rewarding business. Those who are actively involved in the trading of stock and share may find some good news, as there may be gains to be made make from their transactions.

| Main Door | South | Bedroom Sector | Southeast |

農曆五月 (June 5th - July 5th) 壬午

Engineers, technicians and those involved in the technical and engineering professions are likely to find their career prosper this month. Avoid involving in risky investment deals, unless you want to end up with legal problems on your hands. Athletes and sportspersons should be mindful of any sports-inflicted injuries, especially those affecting their legs and feet.

農曆六月 (July 6th - August 6th) 癸未

Those involved in the manufacturing industry will find this to be a productive month, with minimal labour-related problems and maximum profits being the outcomes of the day. This room particularly favour spiritual and religious pursuits this month, so be sure to use this room if you wish to make progress in such endeavours. However, this room is not suitable for those who are already feeling unwell mentally, as the energies will probably going to further aggravate the condition.

農曆七月 (August 7th - September 6th) 甲申

Those using this room will find themselves to be in good health and their relationship thriving harmoniously. Long-term investments are likely to bring considerable profits for those staying in this room. What's more, you will gain respect and recognition from your superior with your prowess and capabilities at work. You may just receive rewards for your exertions!

農曆八月 (September 7th - October 7th) 乙酉

It is advisable to defer any important decision-making related to both personal and professional relationships. It would be hard to be rational and logical when emotions are running high. Be sure to move elderly family members out of this room to prevent the risks of heart disease or even a stroke. Those in the entertainment and electrical business will find this month rather difficult, as demand will not be very encouraging.

農曆九月 (October 8th - November 6th) 丙戌

It is very likely for you to receive the recognition, advancement and financial you have worked so hard to achieve. Investment and merchant bankers who specialize in stocks, equities, and corporate deals and merges will also acquire substantial financial gain on-the-job, so double your efforts if you want more. Couples using this room will prove to be blessed with a harmonious relationship this month.

農曆十月 (November 7th - December 6th) 丁亥

Entrepreneur and those wishing to embark on new ventures should make the most out of the good energy of this room and establish a new start. Those of you working as analysts will also find their career prosper as a result of strategic positioning in the equities market. Mentors and coaches are likely to make their appearance this month, so be sure to take their advice and act on these suggestions to achieve success.

農曆十一月 (December 7th 2020 - January 4th 2021) 戊子

Couples will enjoy a happier relationship this month, and you will do well in your chosen career as well. Both your professional and personal lives will complement each other nicely and leave you feeling contented. However, parents may need to monitor your children and exercise greater authority if necessary, as children using this room are likely to act more rebellious and difficult to control. If your job involves strategic thinking or analysis, be sure to grab the chance to promote yourself, as you will have to chance to advance your career and make a name for yourself this month.

農曆十二月 (January 5th - February 2nd 2021) 己丑

Technical problems will prove to be a problem for those in the cell-phone and communication industries, so be ready to adapt changes and fix what's wrong. In general, people will need to watch their words, as casual or flippant remarks may go down the wrong way and result in unnecessary troubles. Watch out for potential jealousy issues in personal relationship that could cast a shadow over your happiness. This is a situation that requires maturity and tact, so do not respond with jokes or humour.

| Main Door | South | Bedroom Sector | East |

農曆正月 (February 4th - March 4th) 戊寅

Religious enthusiasm could end up in fanaticism for those using this room this month. Financial problems and relationship issues may cause additional stress this month. Those involved in the political arena will find help and assistance from friends and acquaintances with their political aspirations.

農曆二月 (March 5th - April 3rd) 己卯

Conservative property deals are very likely to make good profits but be sure to watch the market carefully. Refrain from taking any unnecessary financial risks. Younger children using this room may face health problems in their ligament, muscles, and tendon. Relationships tend to be on a rocky road this month, so couples using this room should be patient with their loved ones. Losing your temper and being impatient as it could only make things worse.

農曆三月 (April 4th - May 4th) 庚辰

Lawyers will find this month difficult as they have trouble trying to put their case across. Those in the cell phone and IT industry may see losses, as miscommunication will prove to be a problem this month. Be mindful of health issues around the mouth and throat area, as there might be risks of acquiring throat and mouth cancer.

農曆四月 (May 5th - June 4th) 辛巳

Conclusion of deals should be stall or delay until next month if possible, as this is not a very good time for such endeavours. Be mindful of the liver and leg-related injuries and illness this month and keep an eye out for anything amiss. Those in the public relations industry should be careful of miscommunications.

Main Door	South	Bedroom Sector	East

農曆五月 (June 5th - July 5th) 壬午

It is advisable to avoid giving in to the temptation to gamble or engage in any form of speculative investment as you may end up even poorer. Likewise, it is not the right time to embark on a new venture or business, so it'd be best to delay all major decisions. Elderly ladies should be relocated to another room this month, as the risks of acquiring an oral disease or even appendicitis may plague those using this room.

農曆六月 (July 6th - August 6th) 癸未

It is best to stay away from casual relationships this month, as the risks of sexually-transmitted diseases are likely. Be careful when traveling, as this could result in accidents that may require hospitalisation. Ladies using this room should pay more attention to their health, especially to the liver.

農曆七月 (August 7th - September 6th) 甲申

This is not a month to rely on employees, as they are likely to create more trouble than they are worth. So it is better to postpone major projects or ventures that needed the support and teamwork from your staff. It is also advisable to delay major financial deals until a better time, as any deals concluded this month would probably end up being unprofitable. The keywords to survive this month is tolerance and patience. It is unlikely to see a good relationship, so this is not a time to push any arguments.

農曆八月 (September 7th - October 7th) 乙酉

Careful conservative and long-term property deals will come to see the benefit of your investment, in time to come. Those running a family business may want to monitor your employees more closely, to eliminate the risks of being betrayed by disloyal staff. Those using this room should also be careful of possible injuries in their nerves and tendons.

農曆九月 (October 8th - November 6th) 丙戌

Be sure to get the wiring of your property checked out by a qualified electrician or technician. Advocate and solicitor may find it hard to put their points across this month in presenting their case in court. Married couples or couples in a committed relationship may also face problems in their relationship this month. However, don't be unduly frustrated. Just remain calm and patient and keep your wits about you, as you go about executing your duties.

農曆十月 (November 7th - December 6th) 丁亥

Those who are due to sit for an important examination soon should avoid using this room if you do not wish to be distracted. You may also want to be mindful of head injuries or lung ailments this month. Those working in the communication and public relations industries will also find miscommunication proves to be a problem but the issue can be solved by trying to communicate more coherently with other parties. Refrain from making any investment for the time being, as wealth luck is generally poor this month.

農曆十一月 (December 7th 2020 - January 4th 2021) 戊子

Expectant mothers should be refrained from using this room to prevent pregnancy complications. Generally, this is not a favourable month for most important activities. So, it is not a good time to request for a pay-rise or a promotion. Businesspersons should also postpone all major deals for a more favourable period in time.

農曆十二月 (January 5th - February 2nd 2021) 己丑

Be prepared for competition rising in the workplace. Rivalries could increase and jealousy and envy may come to the mix. However, take extreme care not to allow this situation to develop into hostility. If you are not careful enough, legal issues could be the ramifications. It is best to keep a low profile and concentrate solely on your work. Relationships tend to present itself as short-term affairs, so don't invest too much of your time or emotions into it.

Main Door	South	Bedroom Sector	Northeast

農曆正月 (February 4th - March 4th) 戊寅

It is best to avoid dealings in shares and equities, as you may make the wrong choice that you will regret later when it comes to important personal or financial decisions this month, especially when you are unable to see the situation clearly. Expectant mothers should be refrained from using this room, as there may be a risk of pregnancy complications or accidents when traveling.

農曆二月 (March 5th - April 3rd) 己卯

Those using this room will enjoy a romantic month, as long as there is no water outside of this room. If you are involved in any joint ventures and partnerships, beware of any hidden legal entanglements. Those in academia are probably going to receive a much-deserved recognition for their works of literature this month.

農曆三月 (April 4th - May 4th) 庚辰

Business opportunities abroad and offshore will enhance the bottom line this month. Those involved in the furniture business will find to make financial gains this month, however, be wary of potential betrayals and rumours about your business, which could lead to financial loss and legal problems. You may need to watch your back and safeguard your interests as much as possible.

農曆四月 (May 5th - June 4th) 辛巳

Those in the real estate business are likely to find their property deals to return good profits this month! Good financial gains are for you to enjoy at this point. Where else, married couples should be wary of unnecessary third-party gossips, which could cause you some amount of tension in your relationship. Pregnant women should avoid using this room, as there is a likelihood of miscarriages and pregnancy complications.

農曆五月 (June 5th - July 5th) 壬午

It is favourable for you to go get that promotion you had been eyeing for with your inner talents of wisdom and knowledge. Those who are in professional and competitive sports, you are likely to do well in international competition this month using this room. Be mindful of the presence of negative Sha outside of this room, as it could affect the health of the elderly people, in the form of head injuries.

農曆六月 (July 6th - August 6th) 癸未

Those who are in the literary industry should showcase their talent this month if they wish to achieve literary success. Those involved in the professional or competitive sport will also do well this month, and it's the time to maximize your effort as the going is good. Mental instability and emotional stress prove to be a problem this month for those using this room.

農曆七月 (August 7th - September 6th) 甲申

People working in the tourism, travel, logistics and the spa industry are likely to see positive publicity for their business and favourable profit will return as a result. Be sure not to only focus on making money, but spare some time for your partner, as they may feel neglected when you are busy making money. There are some good deals in property investments with good financial rewards to be grabbed, so it's time to try looking around and engage in such deals.

農曆八月 (September 7th - October 7th) 乙酉

Health proves to be a problem for this month, so watch out for signs of unwell especially to the head and mouth. You may want to stay away from romance, as it could only end in tarnished reputation and lowered spirit. Refrain from making a speculative investment this month, otherwise, you will find them turn sour as a result of miscommunication.

農曆九月 (October 8th - November 6th) 丙戌

You will find yourself making progress with personal reputation and gaining recognition at work. So it's time to accept the credit given to you and enjoy it with good grace. Those using this room will also find complicated relationships or estrangement be smoothened out and amicably resolved. Be sure to take up any joint venture opportunity available at this point, as they should end up in good profit in the long run.

農曆十月 (November 7th - December 6th) 丁亥

Avoid dealing with shares and equities this month, as it may cause you some tough challenges. Important personal or financial decisions should also be delayed and postponed, for you could not be able to see the situation clearly, and may end up making the wrong choice that you will regret. Pregnant women should be refrained from using this room to prevent risks of pregnancy complications or accidents when travelling.

農曆十一月 (December 7th 2020 - January 4th 2021) 戊子

Those in the academic industry who use this room will find to receive recognition for their works and writings this month. Beware of any hidden legal entanglement if you are one of those involved in joint ventures and partnerships. Romantic relationships will generally be on the upswing this month, as long as there is no water outside of this room.

農曆十二月 (January 5th - February 2nd 2021) 己丑

Couples will find that relationship will turn strained and filled with disputes and arguments. Be sure to practice tolerance and patience with each other. Aim to alleviate the situation by approaching it calmly, and without reacting to everything emotionally. Make sure that you stay out of office politics and gossip, or it could develop into large-scale problems that no one will be interested to clean up in the end.

Main Door	South	Bedroom Sector	North

農曆正月 (February 4th - March 4th) 戊寅

Fraud and embezzlement by friends and family members will leave you feeling betrayed for those who use this bedroom this month. Those working with heavy machinery should practice extra caution, as there are increased risks of injuries at work. Employees should stay away from office politics, even the petty ones, to prevent unnecessary arguments and disputes which could result in possible legal entanglement.

農曆二月 (March 5th - April 3rd) 己卯

Be careful when you are on the road this month, as there is an increased risk of car accidents. Limit your travel using cars, where possible, walk. Likelihood of recognition, reward, and advancement is high, with the possibility of you being appointed to positions of authority. Family tension should be diffused as much as possible, as there will be disagreements with a figure of authority, such as father, this month.

農曆三月 (April 4th - May 4th) 庚辰

Refrain from gambling activities this month, as it may result in financial loss. Couples using this bedroom should be more patient and tolerant of each other. Avoid blaming the other party, or it could only worsen the situation. Consider moving into another room if you already feel unwell, as the energies in this room will only worsen your condition.

農曆四月 (May 5th - June 4th) 辛巳

Watch out for the possibility of fraud even though underhand transactions are increased this month. Those who suffer from emotional instability or depression should consider moving into another room for the meantime, or at least until things improve. There is a possibility of fame, enhanced reputation and an increase in wealth for those in the company this month, be sure to grab the chance and make the advancement of yourself.

Main Door	South	Bedroom Sector	North

農曆五月 (June 5th - July 5th) 壬午

Be sure to put your personal safety to the top of your priority this month, as there is a likelihood of being robbed or mugged. The good energies in the room will benefit analysts and scientific researchers, provided that there is a good quality mountain outside of this room. Work to improve on family ties and withdraw from family arguments, as disagreements could result in a lawsuit and divide the family into fractions.

農曆六月 (July 6th - August 6th) 癸未

If you are in the fashion or clothing-retail business, this is a good time to expand your enterprise! You will find the opportunity to conclude overseas deals, which could bring you a handsome profit. The energies in this room bode well with academic and educational endeavours and are beneficial to the scholars, academics and those in the literary and artistic field. Couples in a committed relationship who wished to take things to the next level should pop 'the question' this month, as the answer is likely to be favourable.

農曆七月 (August 7th - September 6th) 甲申

Those involved in overseas or offshore business ventures are likely to find windfall gains this month. However, you will need to ensure that necessary internal controls and procedures are in place, to eliminate the risk of fraud or theft as much as possible. For those already feel unwell, you may want to take extra caution on health-wise, as there are risks of internal injuries. Be sure to visit your doctor when the earliest sign of unwell occurs to prevent it from developing to a more serious condition.

農曆八月 (September 7th - October 7th) 乙酉

It is best to avoid traveling for business-related purpose, as the outcome for such a trip will not be favourable to you. If you've been toiling at your job and sense that promotion is just waiting for you, you might just be hitting the nail right on its head! And if it comes, you will be elevated to a well-deserved position with more power, status, and authority. Parents might want to consider moving your teenage son into another room, as you may need to put up with their rebellious attitude even more than usual if they continue staying in this room.

農曆九月 (October 8th - November 6th) 丙戌

Refrain from making any speculative investments or give in to the temptation of gambling activities, unless you wish to risk accumulating huge financial losses. If you had been doing well in financial lately, it is best to remain discreet and prudent on your financial status, or you risk your newly-acquired wealth robbed or stolen away from you. Be mindful of health problems as well, especially issues in the form of ulcers, gallstones or liver-related ailments, and get them treated at the first sign of unwell.

農曆十月 (November 7th - December 6th) 丁亥

Employers may want to monitor their staff or employees closely this month, there's a chance that dishonest individuals or two might up to some hanky-panky at work, or have their hands in the company's 'money jar'. However, this doesn't mean that you should mistrust or distrust all of your staff. Those who make a living from the literary, creative or artistic field will find yourself in good tidings with fame, wider repute, and a fatter bank account. Nevertheless, those suffering from depression or any mental problems may want to consider moving out from this room this month to prevent aggravating their condition.

農曆十一月 (December 7th 2020 - January 4th 2021) 戊子

If you always keep abreast of current trends and stay on top of your 'game', the risks losing your share of the market or even a niche market shall be eliminated. Pay particular attention to communication, as lack thereof could potentially undermine your endeavours. Be mindful of disputes brewing within the family and try to dissolve such situation before it festers into a more serious problem. There is a likelihood of robbery, so be sure to prioritize your personal safety.

農曆十二月 (January 5th - February 2nd 2021) 己丑

Business owners should ensure that all your deals are on the straight and narrow, as otherwise, the chance of encountering losses as results of legally dodgy deals are very high, and it's too steep a price for you to pay simply to cut a few corners. If you do your homework, it is very likely for you will make a successful speculative property investment based on your knowledge on the subject. At the same time, to make romantic relationships work, and thrive, will require that both partners give each the requisite amount of space.

SE	S	SW
6	2	4
5	**7**	9
1	3	8

E ... W

NE ... N ... NW

農曆正月 (February 4th - March 4th) 戊寅

Stagnant career and business are very likely to be revived through making big changes. Try to approach things with a fresh perspective and you might see favourable outcomes. Young children are prone to injuries by sharp metal objects and metal implements, so it is advisable to move them out of this room this month. Do not let your arguments with anyone get out of hand, as these could lead to legal complications.

農曆二月 (March 5th - April 3rd) 己卯

Those of you who are single and looking to start a romantic relationship may be in luck this month! You will find it is very unlikely to be short of potential partners, so be wise when such dealings to prevent complications. Success often breeds contempt and jealousy but it is better to ignore the plots hatched by such individuals to undermine you. This month, it's the time to invest prudently in the property and real estate industry, however, bear in mind that the investment should be made to generate long-term income.

農曆三月 (April 4th - May 4th) 庚辰

This month, health luck is in favour of those using this room, meanwhile, for couples who use this room will find their relationship to be harmonious and happy. Students who die to sit for important examinations should tap into the good energies in the room for good results. Good profits will be obtained from previous investments in shares and equities, but it is advisable to invest your profits to generate even more profits in the future. As they say, 'money makes money'.

農曆四月 (May 5th - June 4th) 辛巳

Those using this room this month will be able to enjoy good news and celebrations, as recognition for something you have succeeded in and promotion is likely as a result. You will finally get to enjoy your fruit of labour. Those wishing to get married should take advantage of the good energies this month and go ahead with the preparations.

Main Door	South	Bedroom Sector	Northwest

農曆五月 (June 5th - July 5th) 壬午

Refrain from engaging in real estate or property deals this month, as there are risks of financial losses. It is advisable to focus on your career and work, rather than be tempted to party and socialize frequently throughout the month. Sportspersons, especially professional athletes, should be mindful of muscle or tendon injuries this month.

農曆六月 (July 6th - August 6th) 癸未

Salaried employees may feel that they are being exploited by their superiors at work, who are only out to make financial gains at the expense of their staff. So, it is only good for you to know when and where to draw the line, and negotiate deadlines and workloads where necessary. Journalists, reporters, and individuals who harbor literary or artistic ambitions will find this to be a good time of the year to pursue their dreams. After all, nothing ventured, nothing gained. Be mindful of the presence of negative features outside this room, as these are may raise the risks of potential back or joint problems.

農曆七月 (August 7th - September 6th) 甲申

In general, this is a stressful time of the year for both professional and personal relationships, so resist the temptation to commit yourself to any major decision about the future. Refrain from engaging in important business negotiations this month, as otherwise, you may risk being entangled in a legal dispute, later. For the boys using this room, be mindful of leg injuries or cuts from a mishap. It is advisable to relocate your young boys or infant sons to another room this month.

農曆八月 (September 7th - October 7th) 乙酉

There will be slow down this month and managers should use this time to motivate and prepare your staff for the next peak ahead. This will also be a quiet month for relationship, so it is better to focus on your career rather than on romance this month. You might make better decisions, plans, and goal setting without having to worry about relationship issues. Be careful of dislocating limbs or tearing ligaments this month.

農曆九月 (October 8th - November 6th) 丙戌

Those in the forestry, dairy or agriculture business will find this a profitable month, but be careful that you do not let your superiors take advantage of you and end up making gains at your expense. It's time to keep your back up and protect your own interest. Possible improved health is in sight this month.

農曆十月 (November 7th - December 6th) 丁亥

This is a favourable time of the year for both personal and professional endeavors, as career advancement, promotion, recognition, and financial rewards beckon to those who deserve them. So if you are looking for the best opportunity to pop 'the Question' to your beloved, now's the time for you to take things to the next level! At the same time, couples looking to conceive and using this room are very likely to receive good news soon.

農曆十一月 (December 7th 2020 - January 4th 2021) 戊子

There is a chance of acquiring handsome profits from speculative real estate investments but make sure that all the details have been taken care of by lawyers, as any legal stone left unturn may cause some problems in the future. Those in authority or of high social status will find that things are in their favour this month so take advantage of any opportunity that comes your way. Elderly women should be mindful of even minor illnesses, especially in the stomach area, to prevent it from developing into something more serious. It is best to visit your doctor as soon as the first sign of something amiss shows up.

農曆十二月 (January 5th - February 2nd 2021) 己丑

Couples using this room may run into some problems and issues this month, so be sure to put in more effort to communicate with each other, and maintain your relationship tie with your partner. Business owners may want to utilise the power of the media at this point to bring a good amount of exposure for you and your business. Generally, those in the public relations, events management, and promotions industries will do well this month, but you will need to be careful of potential fraud or embezzlement that could cost you dearly.

| Main Door | South | Bedroom Sector | West |

農曆正月 (February 4th - March 4th) 戊寅

If you are working in the communication industry, it is a great opportunity for you to widen your network of contact. Be wary with any altercations with the law or confrontation with other parties that would only land you in hot soup as your emotions are rather hostile, aggressive or irritable of late. Inventors should tap into the positive energies of this room to get inspiration and give you the push to make that crucial first step in marketing your latest creation.

農曆二月 (March 5th - April 3rd) 己卯

This may not be a smooth sailing month at the workplace as you might need to deal with disgruntled employees throwing the occasional spanner in the wheel. Be sure to stay focus and nip every problem in the bud before it develops into something more serious. Relationship and health look favourable this month, so make the most of these luck prospects and bend them to your advantage. Those involved in the futures, equities, and stock trading industries need to be alert in taking up any opportunities that come a-knocking.

農曆三月 (April 4th - May 4th) 庚辰

Refrain from concluding major investment deals this month, as they would more likely be loss-generating than profitable. Couples using this room should be more sensitive to each other's feelings and remember not to take each other for granted, as both of you tend to be temperamental and moody this month. Exercise patience and employ tact and understanding in dealing with your partner. Be mindful of the risks of acquiring food poisoning if you noticed any negative features outside this room.

農曆四月 (May 5th - June 4th) 辛巳

Ladies using this room this month are likely to do well at work, especially those in the public relations and marketing field. So be sure that you make the most of this opportunity to further advance your career! A well-planned and shrewdly executed business plan will allow you to gain profit from your endeavours. However, you may need to watch out for rivalry ad competitors from the industries if you are in the education business. Avoid locating the elderly and sick folks in this room, as the energies present here would only further aggravate their health problems, particularly in the liver.

Main Door	South	Bedroom Sector	West

農曆五月 (June 5th - July 5th) 壬午

This month, fortune favors the wise and prudent, so invest wisely and you will see favourable results. However, there might be some domestic or family-related problems occurring this month, it is best if the problem can be dissolved as quickly as possible, to prevent things from festering into a more serious situation. If your job includes counseling or provides psychiatric or psychological treatment, you will be pleased to know that your beneficiaries will appreciate the wisdom, advice, and knowledge you share with them.

農曆六月 (July 6th - August 6th) 癸未

For those who have worked hard and put in an adequate amount of effort, career luck will be favorable throughout the month with possible promotion and advancement prospects. At the same time, those who are single-and-searching for Mr. or Ms. Right will find the energies in this room benefits their search for romance. So be bold to take the initiative. It is best for expectant mothers to stay away from this room to prevent the risks of pregnancy complications.

農曆七月 (August 7th - September 6th) 甲申

Travel opportunities in the name of the business will bring positive financial gains as outcomes of the day, so go ahead and pack your suitcase. Don't forget to make sure that your passport and other travel documents are valid and in order. The energies in the room will benefit those involved in the services and entertainment business, with more customers patronizing their joint in business. Married couples should take this opportunity to go on that long-planned vacation with your spouse, as this is an extremely ideal time to foster even closer ties with your loved one.

農曆八月 (September 7th - October 7th) 乙酉

It is best to eliminate the presence of negative features or structures outside this room to prevent the risks of fire hazards. Have a qualified electrician check the wiring and electrical systems and apparatus in your property promptly to ensure everything is in place. Traveling in the name of business may bring you more revenue this month, especially for those working in the fashion industry. The energies in this room favours spiritual and religious activities this month, so it's time to embark on a spiritual or meditative retreat to cleanse your thoughts and get away from the hullabaloo that is life.

農曆九月 (October 8th - November 6th) 丙戌

It's time to double your effort, especially for politicians and those working in the public/civil service, as this is a favorable month to attain that promotion, career or status advancement, or salary increment that you have been eyeing all this while. This is a good time to look to establish a joint venture or partnership for the budding entrepreneurs. For domestic-wise, happy events and celebrations are very likely, so sit back and enjoy this smooth-sailing month.

農曆十月 (November 7th - December 6th) 丁亥

This is a suitable month to widen your network of contacts for those working in the communications industry, as you only stand to gain by doing so. You may be feeling rather hostile, aggressive or irritable lately but it is advisable to keep a tight rein on your emotions, as any altercations with the law or confrontation with other parties would only land you in hot soup. The positive energies in this room may inspire the inventors to progress with their profession, so don't be afraid to take that all-important step in marketing your latest gadget!

農曆十一月 (December 7th 2020 - January 4th 2021) 戊子

Be wary of the disgruntled employees throwing the occasional spanner, as it could turn out to be a month of 'fire-fighting' at the workplace for you. It's important to stay focused, and nip every problem in the bud before it spins out of control. You will find that relationship and health luck are favourable this month, so don't miss the chance to make use of these luck prospects and bend them to your advantage. Those involved in the futures, equities, and stock trading industries should be vigilant, in seizing any opportunities that come by.

農曆十二月 (January 5th - February 2nd 2021) 己丑

Be wary of gossip arising out of third-party interference1may cause tension in your marriage and relationship. Filter what you listen to, and choose whom you put your trust. Otherwise, you'll have to endure certain problems that will have some long-term repercussions and consequences. You are likely to gain profits from your property investments this month.

農曆正月 (February 4th - March 4th) 戊寅

Travel may bring about greater profits this month, so consider doing it if possible. Generally, this is a good month for property acquisition, but these may produce even better financial rewards if you are required to travel to conclude the deal. Those in the forestry and dairy farming industry will find an increasing demand for their products. Elderly women should be mindful of the risks of acquiring strokes and migraines.

農曆二月 (March 5th - April 3rd) 己卯

There will be some serious disagreements for couples who use this room and where estrangement is present, divorce is likely. Be mindful of unnecessary injuries for the workmen using machinery with sharp blades. Make sure that you scrutinise all legal documents carefully so that legal obligations are thoroughly checked before concluding the relevant deals.

農曆三月 (April 4th - May 4th) 庚辰

Although you might find that concluding deals will require much effort and patience on your behalf, especially when dealing with difficult clients, but these dealings will prove to be a good profit this month. With the presence of harmonious energies in this room this month, relationships are very likely to be able to take on a new level of commitment.

農曆四月 (May 5th - June 4th) 辛巳

This is a good month to consider expanding your business, especially for those working in the management and consultation industries. Likewise, with unlimited inspiration flow, professionals in the literary and media industry will also do well this month. However, couples using this room may find their relationship to be rather tense and strained this month, so it's time to take a break from usual daily undertakings and go on a vacation to clear your minds and forget all your worries.

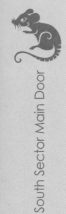

| Main Door | South | Bedroom Sector | Southwest |

農曆五月 (June 5th - July 5th) 壬午

Couples using this room will find wind in their sails this month and will be able to enjoy happiness and growth in their relationship. Be sure to make use of the positive energies in this room to foster closer ties with your loved ones. Those in marketing and consulting will find the opportunity to excel and make a name for yourself through publishing papers or doing some form of intellectual research. This is a good month for leisure travel, so consider booking your holiday tickets early!

農曆六月 (July 6th - August 6th) 癸未

Those in the artistic and creative fields are very likely to do well, especially if they market themselves abroad. Traveling abroad in the name of business will bring greater profits and critical acclaim for your work. It is advisable to stay away from office politics, as there will be unfriendly rivalries that could develop out of control and may lead to unfavourable outcomes. Parents may want to keep a closer eye on their children, as they could be influenced by peer pressure to get involved in rebellious activities.

農曆七月 (August 7th - September 6th) 甲申

Those in the metaphysical fields are likely to find the energies of the room are in favour of embarking on new studies in this field. Be mindful of misunderstanding from offshore business dealings which could end up jeopardising future business relationships. Females using this room may need to take extra care of your health, especially to stomach upsets, ulcers, and gastronomical problems. Be sure to get it treated as early as possible to prevent it from developing into something more serious.

農曆八月 (September 7th - October 7th) 乙酉

Generally, couples using this room should find themselves in a blissful situation that is conducive to good relationships, however, be sure to eliminate the existence of water in this room to avoid chances of infidelity and scandals. The academics are likely to receive good news and good reception to their work, as this month augurs well with paper submission and speeches. Those in the engineering and mining field will find this month benefits them in engaging new deals.

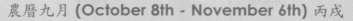
農曆九月 (October 8th - November 6th) 丙戌

Watch your back and mind what you say this month, as malicious people are out for your blood this month. Be careful to not let them use your words against you in the future. Watch out for head or brain-related injuries. This is obviously not something to be taken lightly, or shrugged off easily! Traveling in the name of business may bring those in the artistic and creative success to enjoy.

農曆十月 (November 7th - December 6th) 丁亥

It is likely to realise your returns on investment this month for those actively involved in the real estate and property field. Professionals and enthusiasts dabbling in the metaphysical and esoteric fields will also benefit from the energies of this room, so tap into these positive energies to seek growth this month. The relationship is rather tense between the in-laws, especially if you both live under the same roof. Where possible, avoid contact with your in-laws to sidestep any unnecessary misunderstanding.

農曆十一月 (December 7th 2020 - January 4th 2021) 戊子

For those in the media or consultation industry, this is the month to let your talent shine for all to see, and you shall receive fame, publicity, and recognition for your effort and capabilities. Couples who use this room will find their relationship enhanced, however, make sure that there is no significant water feature outside of this room, as otherwise, it could indicate the possibility of one partner straying, and engaging in an extra-marital affair. This is also a good room to use for students due to sit for important examinations, or academics or intellectuals doing research as part of their job scope.

農曆十二月 (January 5th - February 2nd 2021) 己丑

There will be troubles brewing in your work situation, and it is better not to depend wholly on your employees, as they may cause more troubles than what's worth. It is advisable to delay and postpone all major projects that need sustainable teamwork and support from your staff. Males using this room should be careful of possible legal entanglements, especially those that arise out of car or vehicle accidents. Couples may find this month full of arguments and disrupting the general peace. Be sure to exercise patience and tolerance to each other.

Southeast Sector
Main Door

| Main Door | Southeast | Bedroom Sector | Southeast |

This section contains the monthly outlook for all 12 months of the year for different bedroom sectors, in a property with a Southeast Main Door.

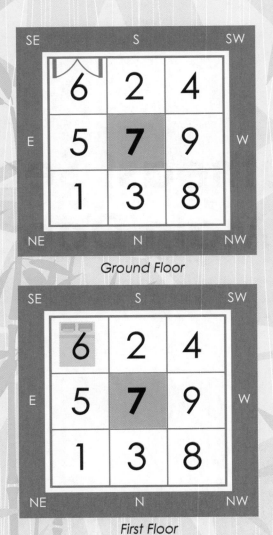

Ground Floor

First Floor

農曆正月 (February 4th - March 4th) 戊寅

Health and relationships are relatively stable this month. Increased profits could be seen for those in the logistics, courier and tourism business. If your job involves strategic thinking or analysis, you will find chances to advance your career and make a name for yourself this month, so be sure to grab the opportunity to enhance your reputation.

農曆二月 (March 5th - April 3rd) 己卯

Those in the entertainment and electrical industry will find that this is a good month for them financially with the executives at the forefront of the gains. Employers should keep an eye on their employees this month, as your staff may be prone to challenging authority and will be somewhat difficult to manage. Elderly males should pay extra attention to their health, especially in regards to blood and lung disease.

農曆三月 (April 4th - May 4th) 庚辰

You are likely to make good financial gains in property investments this month, so don't be afraid to invest! Newly-married couples will find to enjoy a harmonious and blissful relationship this month. As an employee, the recognition and promotion that you have been waiting for are very likely to head to your way this month.

農曆四月 (May 5th - June 4th) 辛巳

It is best to keep a low profile in the workplace this month, as otherwise, you will find competitors challenging in your working field. Also, beware of jealousy from rivalries and colleagues that could result in legal problems if it gets out of hand. Those working with heavy machinery should be more careful of injury while on duty. Couples are likely to face difficulties and a few troubles, as arguments will continue for months.

Main Door	Southeast	Bedroom Sector	Southeast

農曆五月 (June 5th - July 5th) 壬午

Those involved in competitive sport are likely to obtain a good result in competitions as the energies this month are beneficial to such endeavours. Faithful employees will also find their previous effort to come to fruition this month, and long-awaited rewards within the company will materialise. Be mindful that the elderly folks of the household will become stubborn when it comes to health issues this month.

農曆六月 (July 6th - August 6th) 癸未

This room augurs well for spiritual or religious pursuits. So this is the time for you to further your pursuit in such endeavour and receive a better outcome than expected. However, any negative (environmental) forms outside of this room should be avoided, as otherwise, these could be the harbingers of urinary-tract or blood-circulation problems. Manufacturers and producers should make the most of your resources this month to maximize their profits.

農曆七月 (August 7th - September 6th) 甲申

Travel in the name of business this month will very likely to enable you to enjoy a good return, so pack your bag and get ready to embark on your business. It is better for you to remain a low profile for those who are involved in the financial world of stocks, bonds, and anything that involves monetary management. On the domestic front, you may find there is constant bickering among family members that might even lead to legal entanglements! If you happen to be a chronic migraine or headache sufferer, then there's very little you can do but stay clear of these disputes until you're fit enough to deal with them.

農曆八月 (September 7th - October 7th) 乙酉

Financial rewards are likely this month for employees in the engineering field, as a result of gaining support from their superiors. However, there will be an increase in tension between father and son and it would be better to keep children away from this room this month.

農曆九月 (October 8th - November 6th) 丙戌

Those who do their homework and research on speculative investments in the defense industry are very likely to produce good profits this month. It is best to move to another room if you are already feeling unwell, in terms of mental, as mental and emotional instability will plague those using this bedroom this month. The 'well-to-do' will find things going well for them this month with a life that is free of troubles and generally comfortable.

農曆十月 (November 7th - December 6th) 丁亥

This month, politicians will find their policies and stances popular among the masses. Expect some intense business rivalry, accompanied by backstabbing and jealousy at work. It is advisable to keep your emotions under control and be tactful, as any confrontation or argument could well blow-up into epic outcomes. You may want to keep on eye open for your health conditions, especially to kidney-related trouble.

農曆十一月 (December 7th 2020 - January 4th 2021) 戊子

This is a month for possible promotions and salary increment, so if you are planning to hand in such requests to your boss, this is the time! However, be mindful of jealous rivals who may plot to bring you down. Those in the banking, equities or financial industries will find things start rather slow at the beginning of the month, but it will gradually pick up as time goes. Those who were born in the Year of Rabbit may need to pay extra caution on their health as these people are susceptible to flu or any illnesses attacking their respiratory system this month. So, it is advisable to maintain a healthy lifestyle, and consult the doctors at the earliest sign of unwell.

農曆十二月 (January 5th - February 2nd 2021) 己丑

You may find both of your personal and professional relationships are going through a rocky road this month. The underlying reason behind this is probably plain and simple miscommunications. So be sure to talk to others, not about others, and you'll weather the storm quite nicely. It is wise to stay away from any issues that may cause misunderstandings in the workplace, as arguments and disputes are likely to be the norm of this month. Most importantly, make sure you scrutinise all legal documents and contracts before concluding any business deals this month, to avoid the possibility of running into any legal complications later on.

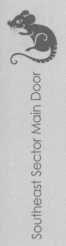

Southeast Sector Main Door

農曆正月 (February 4th - March 4th) 戊寅

Lawyers are probably going to find this a tough month, as they will have trouble putting their case across. Miscommunication will be the main problem of this month, affecting those in the cell phone and IT industry and could cause losses. Likewise, it is also going to affect couples using this room, so it is best to be careful about what is said and what done, which could exacerbate this issue and prolong it for an indefinite length of time.

農曆二月 (March 5th - April 3rd) 己卯

Refrain from making any investment decision this month and maintain a more hand-on approach within the company instead. Business owners should also be careful of disloyal employees this month, as they will use underhanded tactics and deceit to try to undermine your business. Elderly folks using this room should be mindful of head injuries and bone problems.

農曆三月 (April 4th - May 4th) 庚辰

This might be a challenging month for those in the tourism, travel and/or media business. As such, it is better not to make any major decisions this month. Chances are, you would already be in a confused and irritable state of mind, and this doesn't favour for your sense of reasoning and judgment. Pregnant ladies should avoid using this room, as it could result in pregnancy complications.

農曆四月 (May 5th - June 4th) 辛巳

Those using this room this month may want to be mindful of health problems affecting your kidneys or blood circulatory system. For domestic front, couple relationships will be affected, due to possible interference by a third party, and it could lead to major quarrels at home. Those working in the tourism, courier, and logistics will find themselves having to double their effort this month but don't give up just yet.

| Main Door | Southeast | Bedroom Sector | East |

農曆五月 **(June 5th - July 5th)** 壬午

It is advisable for those who are due to sit for major examinations to avoid using this room, as the energies in the room don't favour such endeavours. As such, it is also wiser to refrain from engaging in any significant investment this month, as it is likely to burn a big hole in your financial books.

農曆六月 **(July 6th - August 6th)** 癸未

Miscommunication appears to be the biggest problem of this month, and it could affect both your personal and professional relationships. Therefore, those whose jobs require utilising communication skills will find it rather difficult this month. Lawyers and legal counselors, may want to consider delaying or postponing any litigation cases, as your argumentative and persuasive powers are weak and you may find it very difficult to put your case across this month.

農曆七月 **(August 7th - September 6th)** 甲申

For those using this room, be sure to watch out for office politics this month. Relationships in the workplace seem to be rather tense, so make sure to be careful about your words and actions. For business owners and employers, you may need to look out for betrayal from disloyal staff or subordinates. It is advisable to be mindful of health issues, especially to lung problems and joint pains. It is best to consult a physician at once if you are feeling unwell.

農曆八月 **(September 7th - October 7th)** 乙酉

Refrain from making any speculative investment, position on the stock exchange or gambling this month, as it is likely to result in heavy losses. Those in the political arena will find that their political aspiration will be advance with the help of their friends and acquaintances. However, the relationship between colleagues will be rather tense, as a result of stress in the workplace.

農曆九月 (October 8th - November 6th) 丙戌

Conservative property deals will see to bring financial gains this month, however, be sure to exercise extreme caution throughout the deals. Parents will need to keep a watchful eye to their younger children, as they may have some health problems, especially muscle and tendon injuries. Relations don't seem to be smooth-sailing this month, so it is best to be extra patient with your loved ones and exercise a greater sense of tolerance.

農曆十月 (November 7th - December 6th) 丁亥

Those in the entertainment business or the operator of a pub, disco or bistro may want to keep a closer eye on your finances, especially when it comes to dealing with third parties. Relationships will seem to be story and troubled. Health-wise, be mindful of leg injuries, liver ailments and/or other forms of illness.

農曆十一月 (December 7th 2020 - January 4th 2021) 戊子

It is best not to engage in high-risk ventures this month, especially in property and real estate, as the risks of incurring a huge amount of losses are very high. And by `high-risk' ventures, we are also talking about gambling, games of chance and speculative investments. Be mindful of your health and be sure to seek immediate treatment from your doctor at the first sign of an illness.

農曆十二月 (January 5th - February 2nd 2021) 己丑

Communication flows smoothly this month, and it will lead to an increased sense of contentment and happiness. Couples using this room will see their relationship progress in a harmonious and thriving way this month. If you are due to sit for an important examination or soon to be involved in the academic and scholarly field, it is best to use this room to obtain the optimized outcome. Those in the marketing, consultancy and strategic-planning industry will find your skills and expertise much sought-after this month, so go ahead to prove your worth to the world.

SE	S	SW
6	2	4
5	**7**	9
1	3	8

E ... W

NE ... N ... NW

農曆正月 (February 4th - March 4th) 戊寅

It would be wise for business owners to stay in the back seat and consolidate your position for now, as this month is not a good time to progress your business. Envy is the cause of much friction with couples using this room this month, so you may want to consider moving into another room for the period of the month. Pregnant ladies should also avoid this room as they may encounter risks of pregnancy complications using this room.

農曆二月 (March 5th - April 3rd) 己卯

This room bodes well for academics and exam preparation this month, so it is beneficial to children who use this room to study and bring good results as an outcome. Those working in the ports and transportation field are likely to do well this month, as there will be an increase in terms of profits. Couple using this room will also find their relationship enhanced and enable them to foster a closer tie this month, especially if there is a good mountain located outside of this room.

農曆三月 (April 4th - May 4th) 庚辰

Those in the furniture or publishing industry will find their business prosper this month. Try looking for overseas and offshore business opportunities in particular, as those are going to enhance the bottom line even more. Couples staying in this room may encounter some marital discord this month, so it is best to exercise patience to your partner in order not to further aggravate the tension in the relationship.

農曆四月 (May 5th - June 4th) 辛巳

If you are planning to offload some property from your property portfolio, now it's the time to do so, as it is likely to result in good financial gains. Expectant mothers should, however, avoid using this room, as there is a risk of pregnancy complications. Do not take in remarks or information at face value because, at this point, you are surrounded by people looking after themselves first. It is very unlikely for you to get the most accurate answer.

| Main Door | Southeast | Bedroom Sector | Northeast |

農曆五月 (June 5th - July 5th) 壬午

Those working in the creative industries will find chances to make a name for yourself, get into the limelight and make solid financial profits this month. Those in a committed relationship be wary of temptations this month, as it could result in a tense relationship with your partner. You will find many mentors and helpful force around you this month, so be sure to take advantage of the good energies and take on ambitious endeavours that are certain to be a success.

農曆六月 (July 6th - August 6th) 癸未

This month should prove to be a boon for restaurant owners, as there is a chance of profits. Those who are in the entertainment business, or who are working in the health industry will do well using this room this month. It's time to be proactive and requests for a salary increment and a new position with more authority and status.

農曆七月 (August 7th - September 6th) 甲申

This month is beneficial for relationships, it is suggested to invest time in this partnership as it could bring its own rewards. This is also good timing to sell off some favourable property investment, in exchange for exceptional financial gains. Positive career development will be seen this month for the bankers and financial institution employees, which could lead to a possible pay raise.

農曆八月 (September 7th - October 7th) 乙酉

Romance is in sight this month, but it is likely to turn out to be short-term passionate flings, so it is better not to put your hopes up and expect anything lasting. There should be an improvement in interpersonal relationships among family members and friends, so take this opportunity to foster a closer tie with your loved ones. It is advisable to mind your own business this month because if you meddle in other people's affairs, arguments and ill will rather than gratitude is likely.

農曆九月 (October 8th - November 6th) 丙戌

Politician and public servants are likely to find themselves enjoying excellent public support and rise of ranks in the government or their parties this month. Bear in mind that there might be people out to get you this month, but you will also receive help from the Nobleman Star to achieve your goal. Those of you involved in professional sports and using this room will do well this month in your respective fields or disciplines of sports.

農曆十月 (November 7th - December 6th) 丁亥

It is best for business owners to consolidate their business position this month, as they could find it difficult to make progress in anything. Couples using this room may encounter discords caused by jealousy, so it is advisable to move into another room to avoid further aggravate the problem. Expectant mothers should avoid using this room as well to prevent any pregnancy complications.

農曆十一月 (December 7th 2020 - January 4th 2021) 戊子

Children who will be facing important examinations this month should tap into the positive energies of this room to obtain favourable results, as the energies bode well for academics and exam preparation. As deals increase to provide more profits, those working in ports and transportation will do well financially this month as well. Couples using this room will find their relationship sailing smoothly this month, especially if there is a good mountain located outside of this room.

農曆十二月 (January 5th - February 2nd 2021) 己丑

In general, people should avoid running afoul of the law this month, and conduct their behaviour well in public. Those involved in the field of research and development should avoid making any major decisions this month, as your mind is not at its sharpest, and your ability to think rationally and logically is not at its best. It is advisable for the elderly males to go for a full medical check-up at the first sign of unwell, to prevent minor ailments from developing into something more serious and complicated.

SE	S	SW
6	2	4
5	**7**	9
1	3	8
NE	N	NW

E (left), W (right)

農曆正月 (February 4th - March 4th) 戊寅

There is possible theft and fraud problem this month especially by close friends and family members. Extra financial controls should place this month, even though there may be some windfall gains attained from deals made with offshore partners. Be wary of health problems this month, especially ligament tears and tendon injuries. Make sure you visit a doctor even the injuries in minor to prevent it from developing into something more serious.

農曆二月 (March 5th - April 3rd) 己卯

Be careful when you are on the road this month, as there will be an increased chance of car accidents and travelling mishaps this month. The likelihood of career advancement is high and could result in added power and authority. Males teenagers should consider using a different room as they may be more rebellious this month if continue to stay in this room.

農曆三月 (April 4th - May 4th) 庚辰

This is a good month to conclude sales or purchase of properties/ real estate but bear in mind, be sure to scrutinize the documents and read the fine prints before you put your signature on that dotted line, to prevent future legal complications. Make sure to have your electrical wiring and appliances checked immediately by a qualified electrician to avoid the risk of fire hazards. You may find your relationship is rather tense and strained this month, so it is advisable to keep a tight rein on your emotion. It is always good to take a step back and reevaluate the whole situation before making an important decision.

農曆四月 (May 5th - June 4th) 辛巳

This happens to be a good month for those in the legal profession or those whose jobs require persuasion skills. However, it is better to think before you act, as rushing into making any decision may leave you in regret, later. The risks of encountering accidents are likely this month, so be mindful of your steps in whatever you do, and wherever you go.

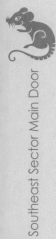

Main Door	Southeast	Bedroom Sector	North

農曆五月 (June 5th - July 5th) 壬午

The energies of the month favours thinking and intellectual pursuits, so be sure to go for it once you have allotted enough thought to a decision. Those children who will be sitting for an examination soon will find this room augurs well for academic and educational activities. Plan carefully and seize every opportunity that comes your way! With the proper timing and stratagem, your efforts will yield satisfactory financial rewards.

農曆六月 (July 6th - August 6th) 癸未

Speculative investment, especially in the property market, is likely to return with good financial gains this month. Relationships will also see improvement, so take advantage of this good time to bring your spouse for a getaway and foster a closer tie. People involved in professional sports should be mindful of legs and feet injuries.

農曆七月 (August 7th - September 6th) 甲申

Those involved in the oil and gas industry should take advantage of good business deals to them this month, as they are most likely to result in good financial gains. Printing and publishing business will also do well this month, with profits coming mostly from overseas sales. Nevertheless, this turns out to be a tough month for relationships. So it is wise to exercise patience and tolerance in your daily undertakings.

農曆八月 (September 7th - October 7th) 乙酉

You may find this month to be a financially challenging month, along with the possibility of betrayals and financial loss. However, those using this room should expect the unexpected, as changes are likely to bring good fortune for those using this room. Those of you working in the travel and travel-related activities will also find good news to come along.

農曆九月 (October 8th - November 6th) 丙戌

Those in the real estate industry will find that they conclude better deals than usual this month, resulting in increased turnover. The fashion and clothing retail business will also make excellent gains this month. So, you can expect to enjoy some good profit if you're involved in those industries. Nevertheless, watch out for certain older people who will try to bring you down because they are envious of your success.

農曆十月 (November 7th - December 6th) 丁亥

It is always good to take in advice from others, especially financial-wise and how you can make your money work for you. However, be sure to filter what you hear and keep your guard up, unless you wish to fall victim to conman or fraudsters. You may find yourself feeling a bit down this, but don't feel too bad. It is natural to feel depressed or sad once a while, but if such symptoms continue, make sure that you seek professional advice.

農曆十一月 (December 7th 2020 - January 4th 2021) 戊子

If you are already suffering from asthma or respiratory illness, it is best to avoid using this room as the energies in the room will only worsen your conditions. Be sure to seek the advice of your physician and continue your medical treatment if you find yourself feeling unwell. You may find some petty-minded, malicious people intended to make your life difficult this month. It is advisable for you to keep a cool head and think before you act, as gossips and conflicts are likely to lead to legal entanglements. All in all, there will be some turbulence this month in your life, but always look forward to better times!

農曆十二月 (January 5th - February 2nd 2021) 己丑

Females using this room this month are most likely to be vulnerable to stress and increasing pressure and tension. You may find your emotions to be a lot topsy-turvier than you'd like! At the same time, be mindful of health problems, especially in the form of ulcers and gastrointestinal issues. The relationship between the in-laws will be rather tense this month, so it is better to minimize contact with each other to avoid creating any undue strains. Consider taking a vacation to ease both your body and spirit, but make sure that you invest in a good form of travel insurance before you embark on your jet-setting adventures!

| Main Door | Southeast | Bedroom Sector | Northwest |

農曆正月 (February 4th - March 4th) 戊寅

Young boys using this room should take extra caution when dealing with any sort of machinery, as there could be injuries to their leg. Relationship this month is quite strained, so it is best to delay and postpone all important decisions about the future to the next month, if possible. To revive stagnant careers and floundering investment, one must make big changes and take bold new steps to resolve this problem.

農曆二月 (March 5th - April 3rd) 己卯

You may be disappointed to find that your efforts are not bearing the results expected. So, take this opportunity to reconsider whether you've been doing things right and the right things now. This turns to be an ideal month to engage in property deals, but make sure that all proper planning has been undertaken if you wish to profit from your investments. Personal relationships seem to be more strained and tense than usual this month. It is advisable to be tactful, sensitive and patient to preserve harmony in your relationships.

農曆三月 (April 4th - May 4th) 庚辰

Those in the communications, public relations and any other industry that requires networking will find this month to be a favourable month for them. You will also find more new opportunities to explore, due to the quick expansion of your network of business. Children using this room will see to develop a sense of independence and responsibility, which could lead to better academic performances.

農曆四月 (May 5th - June 4th) 辛巳

Couples who use this room and looking to start a family are likely to receive good news this month, as the energies are conducive for conception. You are likely to receive recognition for something you have done, for example, publishing a paper in the field of psychology. Romantic relationships turn out to be short-terms flings and passionate romances this month, so it is wise not to invest high hope of it becoming anything long-term.

Main Door	Southeast	Bedroom Sector	Northwest

農曆五月 (June 5th - July 5th) 壬午

It is advisable that business owners should not overemphasize the need to arrest any decline in profit margins, as this could only be stressing-out and de-motivating your employees unnecessarily. Romance luck is not likely to be on your side this month, so it is better to spend your energy and effort on other more rewarding endeavours.

農曆六月 (July 6th - August 6th) 癸未

Excellent commercial opportunities favours to those in the marketing and consultation industries with corresponding financial gains this month. If you have plans to cash in some properties off your properties portfolio, now it's the time to do so, as the return will be satisfying. Those who use this room this month will be blessed with strong academic luck, which is beneficial self-improvement or any other course that will add to your existing repertoire of skills!

農曆七月 (August 7th - September 6th) 甲申

Rewards and recognition from superior are likely to come to those using room and involved in the banking and finance industries this month. Likewise, people in the competitive sport will also gain possible fame and recognition through success in their international activities. However, you will need to be mindful of illness, where kidney problems are concerned.

農曆八月 (September 7th - October 7th) 乙酉

Employees will find that they are stressed out by the stepped-up pressure from their superior, which initiated to push them to perform and increase their expectations. It is better to adopt a more conservative approach to wealth management and investment this month, as this could be a difficult month to make profits. Injury is possible, especially through over-exertion, for athletes and long-distance runners. Therefore, extra caution should be paid when it comes to such concerns.

農曆九月 (October 8th - November 6th) 丙戌

Those using this room will find this month a pleasant and productive one. Those in the travel and construction industry will find substantial profits to be made from their business. This is also a good time of the year to engage in speculative investments, as the return could be favourable. However, you will need to know when to stop engaging in such investments, to gain from them. Couples using this room will find their relationship harmonious and thriving.

農曆十月 (November 7th - December 6th) 丁亥

The positive energies of this room are beneficial to couples trying to conceive and those looking to propose to their loved ones. If you've worked hard all along and believe that you deserve a promotion and salary increment, go ahead and ask your boss for one. Just remember to catch your boss at a good time though.

農曆十一月 (December 7th 2020 - January 4th 2021) 戊子

If there is natural water outside this room, financial gains are possible this month for property dealers and real estate agents. If you are born in the Year of the Goat, you may want to be careful of rivals, subordinates, and colleagues who look to undermine you this month. Elderly women using this room may need to pay extra attention to your health and be alert for any potential of having niggling stomach issues.

農曆十二月 (January 5th - February 2nd 2021) 己丑

Make sure that you get all your electrical wiring and gas outlet thoroughly checked to eliminate the risk of fire hazards. Don't be careless and negligent with these things, or a serious problem could occur. People in the marketing and consultancy business will find this a favourable month, as higher profit margins are in sight. This is likely to be due to your expanded network of contacts, so nurture these professional relationships to the best of your ability. Be watchful of your personal relationship, as there will be a potential for betrayal if a third party enters the picture.

| Main Door | **Southeast** | Bedroom Sector | **West** |

農曆正月 (February 4th - March 4th) 戊寅

This is a good month to request that promotion and seek to advance your career further this month. Strong academic luck is in sight for those using this room as well. Relationships are generally positive and harmonious, as long as there is no natural water formation outside this room.

農曆二月 (March 5th - April 3rd) 己卯

Those using this room may be aggressive and temperamental this month. It is advisable to mind your behaviour while you are in public or at work as it may cause you troubles if you don't control yourself. Be sure to get your wiring checked by a professional electrician to eliminate the risk of fire hazards caused by short-circuits.

農曆三月 (April 4th - May 4th) 庚辰

Much good news and happiness will come to those who use this room this month. Financial gain is also on the cards, especially for those in property development or real estate.

農曆四月 (May 5th - June 4th) 辛巳

It is best for you to keep a close eye on what your competitors are up to. If you let your guard down, you may well find your company the target of a hostile takeover. So be vigilant, although this should not stop you from promoting your products or services aggressively, or embarking on an intensive marketing campaign of your company, as the mass media will provide you with the desired positive exposure. Married men or guys in a committed relationship are advised to be faithful to your other half and instead of giving in to temptation!

| Main Door | Southeast | Bedroom Sector | West |

農曆五月 (June 5th - July 5th) 壬午

Your earlier investments will find to return with substantial gains this month, so now's the time to cash in on them. Be sure to drive carefully this month and make sure all necessary insurance policies are up-to-date, as there are risks of a travel-related mishap. It is advisable for the employers to expect your subordinates to challenge or question your authority this month. Nevertheless, seek first to understand the grievances of your staff, before you make yourself understood.

農曆六月 (July 6th - August 6th) 癸未

Nothing good seems to come out of using the bedroom this month. For example, tempers will flare, and those involved in speculative endeavours and using this room will suffer mental agony, anxiety and financial loss. Pregnant ladies should also avoid using this room, as it could result in miscarriage or pregnancy complications!

農曆七月 (August 7th - September 6th) 甲申

You will be earning the recognition of your superior and colleagues through your diligence and commitment to your job. Be sure to use this to your advantage by expanding your network of contacts to bring you financial and monetary rewards. Women, in particular, who worked in the marketing, public relations and sales industries will find it a very rewarding month. However, bear in mind that the fact that you're a successful career woman though does not justify your dominating or treating your partner or spouse poorly.

農曆八月 (September 7th - October 7th) 乙酉

If your employer is going through a financially-challenging period lately, it is best for you to be a little more patient in expecting any career advancement. The energies here will be favourable to academic and scholar pursuits, so for students who are due to sit for important examinations, they should tap into the positive energies of this room to achieve a better result. However, beware of the presence of any significant body of water within or beyond this room, as it might cause couples to stray or be tempted by another party outside their relationship.

農曆九月 (October 8th - November 6th) 丙戌

Those using this room this month are likely to receive recognition for your effort and capabilities by the others. Those working in the travel, tourism or engineering industries will find this to be a profitable month, so be sure to make hay while the sun shines. Those who are in a steady, committed relationship should use this room more often to foster even closer ties with your loved ones.

農曆十月 (November 7th - December 6th) 丁亥

This room augurs well in business expansion or diversifies your area of commercial operations this month. Work hard, expand your network of contacts, and you should be able to enjoy the rewards of your labours in due time. What's more, do take every opportunity to travel as much as possible, as those who do so will enjoy favourable financial luck this month. Be mindful of ant sharp or negative features outside this room, as the presence of such features indicates the increased risks of heart disease or eyes problems.

農曆十一月 (December 7th 2020 - January 4th 2021) 戊子

If you work as a salesperson or if your work involves intensive sales and marketing, double your efforts, and pursue every business opportunity that comes your way! The energies in this room favour meditative and spiritual pursuits, so this is the room you should use if you are looking to attain a balanced life this month. Children or students will also benefit from the energies of this room, as it augurs well for academic luck as well.

農曆十二月 (January 5th - February 2nd 2021) 己丑

For those involved in the real estate business, this will be a good month for concluded deals that are likely to be profitable. Be sure to put on your skeptic's cloak, especially when people seem overly helpful in sharing information with you at this point in time. Now it's not the time to accept anything at face value, as you are most probably surrounded by people who are only looking out for their own interest now. Expectant mothers should avoid using this room to prevent any possible pregnancy complications.

Main Door	Southeast	Bedroom Sector	Southwest

農曆正月 (February 4th - March 4th) 戊寅

Those involved in agriculture, forestry or dairy farming will find this month to be a bumper month, and it augurs well to further their name in that particular field or even buy new farms. Elderly folks using this room may need to exercise extra caution this month, as the chances of encountering risks of stroke or arterial blockage related to circulation this month are high. Couples using this room are likely to face marital problems as well, so it is advisable to give each other more breathing space. Perhaps, travelling together is a way of resolving such discord.

農曆二月 (March 5th - April 3rd) 己卯

Those who make a living from your artistic and creative talents may find the need to travel this month to earn your keep, but it will be worth the while ultimately. Expectant mothers should avoid this room at all costs to minimize the risks or pregnancy complications and miscarriage. For females that looking for love this month, be sure to select your potential partner carefully. After all, you certainly wouldn't want to fall for a guy with a shady personality, would you?

農曆三月 (April 4th - May 4th) 庚辰

If you find your kids to be more rebellious and prone to picking fights with others, you may want to consider relocating them to another room this month, to prevent them from engaging continuously in some form of unfriendly or unhealthy rivalry. Nevertheless, those seeking a new romantic interest will find this month to be ideal enough to pursue the person who's caught their eye. This room will prove to be beneficial to artistic and creative people, particularly if they are seeking to market their skills abroad.

農曆四月 (May 5th - June 4th) 辛巳

Refrain from involving yourself in the stock market, as the volatility could result in potentially severe financial losses. It is advisable for the couples to allow each other space and be tolerant of each other, as relationships tend to be strained and tense this month. Women using this room should be mindful of the risk of acquiring breast cancer. It is best to get a thorough check-up and mammogram to be certain on the condition of your health.

Main Door	Southeast	Bedroom Sector	Southwest

農曆五月 (June 5th - July 5th) 壬午

This is a favourable month in terms of concluding new deals, especially if you are working in the engineering or mining industry. If you wish to publish a new research paper or academic work and get recognition and acknowledgment for your efforts, this is probably the best month to do so. Romantic interludes will also meet with success. Be mindful of the presence of any significant water forms or features outside this room, as these could be the harbingers of trouble.

農曆六月 (July 6th - August 6th) 癸未

Marital relations tend to show signs of tension and strained this month, so be sure to practice tolerance to your partner to avoid further aggravate the problem. It is better to stay away from any form of office politics, as there will be unfriendly and unhealthy rivalries who may plot to bring down and escalate out of control. Those using this room should be mindful of head and brain injuries this month.

農曆七月 (August 7th - September 6th) 甲申

Those looking to sell their house or buy one should tap into the positive energies of this bedroom to optimize their chances. This sector also augurs well for students or anyone due to sit for important exams soon. Now, if you happen to be involved in the literary, media or engineering industry, take every opportunity to travel as much as possible. You'll find the outcomes from your travels to be financially rewarding.

農曆八月 (September 7th - October 7th) 乙酉

This turns to be a good month for married couples and newly-weds who use this room, as their relationship will become cozy and harmonious. Those in the literary field who wished to put out new work should look for publishers this month, as it could very well result in fame and fortune for you. Those who are due to sit for important examinations this month should use this room to sleep in or to study to benefit from the good energies.

農曆九月 (October 8th - November 6th) 丙戌

If you wish to formalize your relationship, this will be a very good month to do so. You will also find your reputation and honour to be enhanced, so it's time to promote yourself aggressively. If you are expecting to finalize deals in the entertainment industry this month, you should take advantage of this as the outcomes will move in your favour.

農曆十月 (November 7th - December 6th) 丁亥

This is not a very good month for most endeavours. Refrain from making investments in real estate or property, as you'll only stand to suffer losses from such investments. It is best for couples to give some breathing space to each other as marital bliss will be absent from the map this month. Look out for any negative features in the rooms, as it could indicate the risk of acquiring an infection or worse still, liver or breast cancer.

農曆十一月 (December 7th 2020 - January 4th 2021) 戊子

Be mindful of injuries whilst handling blades or sharp instruments. If your jobs involve working on heavy machinery, extra care should be taken not to injure yourself on duty. Females using this room should also be careful of respiratory problems and spinal injuries. Those in the furniture and paper and packaging business will do well this month but be sure to scrutinize all fine prints and detail when signing documents, as this could lead to legal complications.

農曆十二月 (January 5th - February 2nd 2021) 己丑

It is best to move students who are due to sit for important examinations this month to another room, as otherwise they will be easily distracted. For professional sportspeople and those participating in competitive sports, it would be better to focus on improving your skills this month. This could be a rather difficult month in many aspects for those who are required to travel to make a living, especially if you hold positions of authority in your career.

SE	S	SW
6	2	4
5	**7**	9
1	3	8

E ... W

NE ... N ... NW

農曆正月 (February 4th - March 4th) 戊寅

Those who stay in this room will be prone to mental and emotional problems, especially if you are already feeling unwell. Those who are sensitive to the changes in energies in their environment might have a problem this month. Real estate ventures may result in beneficial outcome but it will inevitably take its toll in the form of stress.

農曆二月 (March 5th - April 3rd) 己卯

This is not a very good time to invest or conclude business deals, as these will end up with major losses. You will find obstruction in all areas, no matter how conservatively you run your business. Don't worry, and consider lying low to let the worst of it pass you by. Be mindful of appendicitis or pregnancy complications as well.

農曆三月 (April 4th - May 4th) 庚辰

It turns out this month doesn't bode well with endeavours that involve strategic thinking and decision-making. Be careful when someone makes you an offer that appears too good to be true. Avoid concluding deals or signing contracts this month, so that you will not end up worse off than you first started. Students sitting for exams shouldn't use this room to study as well, as the energies could affect one's ability to think clearly. All in all, do not make any major decisions if you are using this room this month.

農曆四月 (May 5th - June 4th) 辛巳

That much-awaited promotion and pay-raise might just be yours in no time. However, you may find yourself prone to respiratory illness this month, so be sure to do whatever it takes to prevent yourself from falling sick. Likewise, this health alert goes out to all pregnant ladies who are currently sleeping in this room. You may want to relocate to another bedroom this month to avoid even the remotest possibility of a miscarriage or pregnancy complications. Nevertheless, this is not an entirely inauspicious month for everyone and everything. Take this opportunity to network more and expand your list of contacts. It might just pave the way for that business 'opening' that you've always wanted.

Southeast Sector Main Door

農曆五月 (June 5th - July 5th) 壬午

You will find a good opportunity and openings to make money made available for you this month. The key to success lies in not allowing yourself to get carried away and eventually surrender to stress. Romance luck is in sight for the singles this month, however, you also need to keep an eye on your business to prevent from being distracted from the other important facets of your life.

農曆六月 (July 6th - August 6th) 癸未

Watch out for rivals who try to deceive you into deals that will not be financially sound. So be careful of all business dealings this month to keep your business safe. Don't be deceived easily by deals that are too good to be true, as otherwise, these could cost you a fortune, or in the worst case, land you in legal entanglement. Couple using this room will need to look out for potential discord in marriage and family disharmony.

農曆七月 (August 7th - September 6th) 甲申

Refrain from partnerships or joint ventures, as things are not good this month and it is unlikely to result in favourable outcome. Stubbornness and a lack of logical thinking will cause you to make some bad decisions that are likely to result in financial losses. Those staying in this room should be mindful of eye problems. Seek medical treatment immediately if you feel anything amiss.

農曆八月 (September 7th - October 7th) 乙酉

Large investment in property and real estate will result in favourable financial return. So it's time to stick your neck out and make some extra money. Those in the upper social circles of society will find that this month brings with it plenty of opportunities to rub shoulders with the rich and famous. Married couples should be careful that their spouse is not seduced by wealthy people who are out to only have a good time.

農曆九月 (October 8th - November 6th) 丙戌

Surgeons will find that their skills are much sought-after this month. Working parents may need to pay extra attention to their children, as they are likely to bring troubles and difficulties if left unsupervised. Increased competition will be seen in the workplace, which is caused primarily by women, and this could result in arguments and disputes.

農曆十月 (November 7th - December 6th) 丁亥

You may find some handsome gains through real estate and property deals investment this month. However, your relationship turns to be on the downside and it is rather strained and tense between you and your partner. So it is advisable to be sensitive and tactful in dealing with him or her. Drive safely this month, as there's a risk of getting involved in a traffic accident due to reckless driving.

農曆十一月 (December 7th 2020 - January 4th 2021) 戊子

This is a good month to put your money into property or real estate investment, so be bold and select the best property that will guarantee you maximum Returns-on-Investment (ROI). However, students and expectant mothers should avoid using this room, as the energies here will leave an unfavourable effect on these people.

農曆十二月 (January 5th - February 2nd 2021) 己丑

The energies of this room bode particularly well for newly-burgeoning romantic relationships! So males who are looking for a new relationship are likely to meet a compatible new partner this month. It is always good to listen to others and take in experts' advice, especially when dealing with financial investment topics. Those working in the media and travel industries may find this a good month for achievements, honour and boosting of reputation.

Northwest Sector
Main Door

| Main Door | Northwest | Bedroom Sector | Northwest |

This section contains the monthly outlook for all 12 months of the year for different bedroom sectors in a property with a Northwest Main Door.

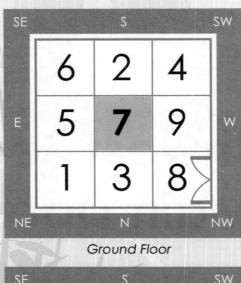

Ground Floor

First Floor

農曆正月 **(February 4th - March 4th)** 戊寅

Adults using this room should focus on academic activities or self-improvement as that is likely to result in personal growth. Children should be careful when using sharp metal objects and implements as risk of injuries is high. Do not make any important business decisions this month as these will not be in your favour and may end in losses.

農曆二月 **(March 5th - April 3rd)** 己卯

There should be success and superior profits for those in real estate industry. This is especially the case if there is water body externally. Those who wish to take their relationship to the next level should do so this month and make use of its favourable energies. However, older women who use this sector this month should not leave minor stomach ailments untreated because these could develop into something more serious.

農曆三月 **(April 4th - May 4th)** 庚辰

This month promises substantial returns-on-investment, especially for those involved in the media and entertainment industry. Similarly, young and budding entrepreneurs should take the opportunity to foray into the market this month, as chances are, you'll be off to a good start. There's also no harm in buying a lottery or lotto ticket; this might just be your lucky month. Just be reminded not to gamble off your savings, as this doesn't necessarily guarantee an absolute win.

農曆四月 **(May 5th - June 4th)** 辛巳

Hardworking employees will finally see their efforts paid off at work, attaining a higher position and increased income. However, they need to be equally mindful of jealous colleagues who are out to sabotage their efforts. Those interested in starting up their own business should try to do so this month by tapping into the energies of this sector. Mentors, life coaches and professionals in the self-help and motivational fields will find their advice benefiting others this month, especially if they make the effort to initiate changes in their own personal lives.

| Main Door | Northwest | Bedroom Sector | Northwest |

農曆五月 (June 5th - July 5th) 壬午

Couples using this room will find their relationship to be harmonious and smooth sailing. What's more, wealth luck smiles upon those using the room this month. The presence of any water features in this sector will enhance your wealth prospects even further. You may consider engaging in some form of speculative but viable investment. However, salaried workers and employees may find themselves feeling stressed due to the increased amount of pressure to perform imposed upon them by their superiors. Keep in mind to manage your work-life balance carefully.

農曆六月 (July 6th - August 6th) 癸未

This is a good month to invest in property so if you have been eyeing that dream house that recently caught your attention, you can now enjoy your new home in no time. However, you should not rush into concluding any type of deal, as you need all the facts and information at your disposal before you can make the final decision. Salaried employees should be mindful of superiors, who are out to profit at their productivity and expense by exploiting them.

農曆七月 (August 7th - September 6th) 甲申

Chaos and unexpected changes may plague your business or venture this month resulting in unbudgeted losses. Therefore, where possible, postpone all deals to a more suitable period in time. However, stagnant careers and flailing enterprises may still be revived or resuscitated if you're prepared to make drastic changes to your business where necessary.

農曆八月 (September 7th - October 7th) 乙酉

The energies of this room bode well for those who desire to take their relationship to the next level; so tap into them accordingly if that's what you seek. Be vigilant for any lucrative property deals headed your way. When opportunities come, seize them at once! On the other hand, elderly women using the room should guard against any potentially chronic stomach ailments this month. Seek doctor's advice at the first sign of trouble.

農曆九月 (October 8th - November 6th) 丙戌

Professionals in the travel and construction industries will find their profit margins significantly improved this month. This is also an ideal month for fund or investment managers and those dabbling in investment portfolios to cash in on their investments as well. Additionally, couples using the room will find their relationship to be easygoing and harmonious. As such, those looking to conceive should use this sector more frequently!

農曆十月 (November 7th - December 6th) 丁亥

This is a suitable time to seek the recognition you deserve; perhaps by publishing that paper or thesis you've labored on for some time. Those using the room this month can expect good news and happy events. Couples looking to start a family should use this bedroom as the energies are favourable.

農曆十一月 (December 7th 2020 - January 4th 2021) 戊子

It's a good time for singles to play the field this month. However, any flings you encounter will remain what they are, so don't expect them to develop into anything long-term or solid. If you happen to be using this bedroom, be more sensitive towards your partner's feelings to preserve domestic harmony and prevent arguments from escalating. There may be profits to be gained from real estate or property investments. But then again, the scales of fortune could just as easily tip against you.

農曆十二月 (January 5th - February 2nd 2021) 己丑

Business owners might get the chance to enjoy increased publicity in the press; capitalise on this opportunity to expand your business further, whether it's through more contacts or revenues. This month, married men should put a check on their roving eyes, as being tempted could lead to something serious – which is exactly what you don't want. Dabbling in an extra-marital dalliance will likely result in dire consequences in your marriage. So, if your ties of matrimony are important to you, steer clear out of any sort of trouble.

Main Door	**Northwest**	Bedroom Sector	West

農曆正月 (February 4th - March 4th) 戊寅

For those in the academic or scholarly research fields, this is a good month to improve your reputation and status in the field. There is the possibility of commercialising an idea or your research this month. If you are applying for a grant for research, using this room will also aid you in successfully obtaining the grant.

農曆二月 (March 5th - April 3rd) 己卯

Those in the fashion industry will find that travel brings about favourable news this month. If you sleep in this bedroom, use this month to make decisions about your investment portfolio or those that involve financial matters as thinking will be lucid.

農曆三月 (April 4th - May 4th) 庚辰

The energies of this room are especially favourable for those of you who wish to develop spiritually, mentally or religiously this month. Budding politicians and seasoned ones should also take this opportunity to take on their rivals or opponents and make their cause known to the highest powers in the government. This is also an ideal time to engage in speculative deals.

農曆四月 (May 5th - June 4th) 辛巳

If you specialise in the fashion and hairdressing businesses, you should capitalise on the publicity given to you in the mass media to promote your services and skills to generate more revenue. Your relationship undergoes the occasional rough patch, but this is no excuse to indulge in an illicit or extra-marital affair. Women should avoid using the room this month, as they are particularly susceptible to eye issues or gallstones if they do so.

Main Door	Northwest	Bedroom Sector	West

農曆五月 (June 5th - July 5th) 壬午

Those finding it necessary to travel in order to conclude their deals will likely reap the rewards of their efforts in due time. Take care of your health as respiratory problems and hemorrhoids may afflict those using the room this month. At work, hold your tongue instead of gossiping about the affairs of others. Unsolicited advice will not be appreciated.

農曆六月 (July 6th - August 6th) 癸未

Expectant mothers using this room are advised to consult their gynecologist for potential pregnancy complications. This is also not the best of time to engage in speculative investments as they will likely result in financial losses. Keep a low profile in both the professional and personal aspects of your life. Otherwise, you would only cause yourself troubles and distress.

農曆七月 (August 7th - September 6th) 甲申

Guard against food poisoning this month, especially if there is any negative features or structures outside this room. Those using this bedroom will also find themselves more temperamental and aggressive towards others. Therefore, be sure to exercise patience and think before you act or say anything. You should also refrain from making any important decisions this month.

農曆八月 (September 7th - October 7th) 乙酉

If you are sitting for major examinations soon, you should make use if this sector to achieve good results. Similarly, couples will find their relationships going well this month due to the positive energies in this room. However, be forewarned that the energies of the room could also pose health issues in the form of eye or heart ailments or even strokes, especially if there is presence of a negative feature outside this sector.

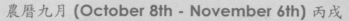

農曆九月 (October 8th - November 6th) 丙戌

Counsellors and coaches will find their skills and advice highly sought-after this month. Share your wisdom and knowledge well so that others may benefit from them. The room is also favaourable for couples looking to conceive. There are also chances for travel for those using the room this month, so make sure you are well-prepared!

農曆十月 (November 7th - December 6th) 丁亥

This will be a turbulent month as tempers and impatience threaten to wreck your relationships and dealings with others. Keep your wits about you and use your head to handle yourself. It would be wise to stay away from discos, nightclubs and places of ill-repute as your visits there will affect your relationship with your loved ones negatively. Pregnant women using the bedroom should also take good care of their health to minimise the risk of miscarriage.

農曆十一月 (December 7th 2020 - January 4th 2021) 戊子

Auspicious news and celebrations are in store for those using this room! Students are likely to excel with flying colours in their examinations. This is also a good time of the year to embark on your business trips as their outcomes will very likely be profitable and successful. Those employed in the services industry will be pleased to find their customer base increasing this month with substantial financial returns.

農曆十二月 (January 5th - February 2nd 2021) 己丑

Plenty of opportunities will come to people in the construction industry and literary field this month. Those in travel and logistics businesses will also benefit from the proliferation of new opportunities. This will be a good time to strike new deals and forge alliances with business partners or associates abroad. In terms of investment opportunities, you will likely enjoy a good agreement and be able to seal the deal. If you are single and looking for your Mr. or Ms. Right, this room bodes well for you on the relationship front this month!

| Main Door | **Northwest** | Bedroom Sector | Southwest |

農曆正月 (February 4th - March 4th) 戊寅

Business owners should ensure that all their dealings are above-board, as they stand to incur huge losses in addition to violating the law by engaging in any illegal deals. Avoid indulging in gambling or any form of speculative investment as you could well end up losing all you have! Women might want to go for a full medical check-up or even a mammogram this month, as there's a risk of acquiring breast cancer due to the energies of the room.

農曆二月 (March 5th - April 3rd) 己卯

Those using this sector to study for their exams or engage in other academic endeavors will find their efforts yielding positive outcomes. Businesswomen should try to venture abroad in securing their deals, as chances are, these will bring them considerable profits in time to come. However, asthma, bronchitis and health problems affecting the lungs and respiratory system may well be the bane of those using the bedroom this month. Seek medical advice and treatment at the first sign of trouble.

農曆三月 (April 4th - May 4th) 庚辰

This is a good month to consolidate both personal and professional relationships or possibly even discuss a long-term future together with your partner. Travelling will bring about an improvement in your stature, reputation or name in your industry or field this month. You'll also find yourself expanding your network of business contacts. Those who work in the mining industry, the stock exchange or trade in financial information will find this is to be a good month in financial terms.

農曆四月 (May 5th - June 4th) 辛巳

If you're traveling this month, ensure that all the necessary insurance policies are in order, in case you encounter unexpected hiccups during your travels. You might also encounter problems communicating with your in-laws. Hence, for the meantime, it's best to minimise any form of contact with them whilst exercising patience in dealing with them. Stomach ailments and ulcers are likely to affect your health this month if you are using this room.

| Main Door | Northwest | Bedroom Sector | Southwest |

農曆五月 (June 5th - July 5th) 壬午

Those in the mining and engineering industries should be able to reap substantial profits this month. Couples using the room should find the energies of this sector conducive to their relationship. However, take note if there is any water feature in this room as this could cause infidelity and scandals! For singles, this is a good month to play the field, but any flings you encounter will not likely develop into anything long-term or serious.

農曆六月 (July 6th - August 6th) 癸未

Any deal concluded this month will be beneficial in terms of the lucrative investment potential it presents. Those in the services and property industries will find this time of the year to be ideal for seeking promotion and recognition. Relationships will be thriving and smooth-sailing this month. If you're looking to embark on a joint venture, go for it, as you stand to give your enterprise a good start!

農曆七月 (August 7th - September 6th) 甲申

Management consultants and professionals in the real estate and property fields will find the energies of the room conducive towards generating revenue from their business. However, you need to beware of health issues such as back and spinal problems if you are using this bedroom as such health risks will be heightened this month.

農曆八月 (September 7th - October 7th) 乙酉

You're advised to scrutinise all legal documents carefully before committing yourself to them, to sidestep the possibility of any legal complications later on. For those in committed relationships, serious disputes and misunderstandings may flare up. Be mindful of your partner's feelings to prevent your relationship from falling apart. Also, those working in industrial or construction sites should prioritise safety and guard against injuring their limbs at work.

農曆九月 (October 8th - November 6th) 丙戌

Your relationships will be elevated to the next level as the energies of this room bode well for fostering closer ties with other parties. Athletes and sportspersons involved in competitions or tournaments should find this a promising month in their quest for gold. However, you may need to be extra careful in concluding your share or equities deals, as difficult clients may cause unexpected delays.

農曆十月 (November 7th - December 6th) 丁亥

If you want to buy or sell your house and are using this bedroom, this is a beneficial time to do so. If you're in agriculture, forestry or dairy farming, you should use this month to further your name in your particular field, as you are likely to receive recognition. If you have written a book, you should try to find a publisher this month as it will bring good reputation and financial gain.

農曆十一月 (December 7th 2020 - January 4th 2021) 戊子

Those in the furniture business will do well, but you need to be extra vigilant when signing documents as this could have legal implications. It is better to be safe than sorry right now. People using this room should also beware of injuries caused by sharp metal objects. If you are interested in meditation or spiritual development, you could use the room this month for further progress.

農曆十二月 (January 5th - February 2nd 2021) 己丑

Those of you with children will be dealing with slightly more rebellious spirits than normal – don't lose your patience and temper too quickly. There will also be plenty of disputes and conflicts requiring your arbitrary and mediating skills. Use your wit and ingenuity to resolve them, and your reputation also enjoys a boost. Be careful of potential car accidents this month, so be extra-cautious when you're on the move.

農曆正月 (February 4th - March 4th) 戊寅

If you're a salaried worker, be careful about being drawn into a dispute or argument at work, which could result in legal entanglements. Use this room especially if you're religiously or spiritually inclined, for such pursuits. Nevertheless, be forewarned that marital problems could arise if you use the room too frequently this month.

農曆二月 (March 5th - April 3rd) 己卯

The women of the household will find themselves more susceptible to stomach and other ailments plaguing their digestive system. Seek immediate medical treatment at the first sign of trouble. Medical practitioners will, however, find their skills much sought-after this month. If you're the gambling type, there's no harm in buying a lottery ticket or playing the sweepstakes this month. Just don't use up every penny at your disposal to win big.

農曆三月 (April 4th - May 4th) 庚辰

Those in property-related fields will reap the rewards for their hard work in the months to come. Academics and scholars will benefit from the good energies of the room this month if they are taking important examinations. This is a good time for self-cultivation and if the opportunity arises, they should take a course for self-improvement.

農曆四月 (May 5th - June 4th) 辛巳

Ensure that all traffic fines and outstanding taxes are up-to-date. Otherwise, you will be overwhelmed by the revenue offices throughout the rest of the month. Though, this is a good sector for those who wish to become involved in religious or spiritual endeavours. If you're a parent with a son using this bedroom, you will have to be prepared for him to be more difficult and argumentative this month.

農曆五月 (June 5th - July 5th) 壬午

Real estate and property developers stand to acquire great wealth from their investments this month. Women should be mindful not to indulge in illicit or scandalous affairs as these will only sully your reputation when what you previously thought you could hide becomes public knowledge. Those using this room are particularly susceptible to head and brain problems, so consider relocating yourself from this sector this month.

農曆六月 (July 6th - August 6th) 癸未

Doctors and physicians will find their skills much sought-after, thanks to their reputation and good name, rather than the incidence of more people falling ill this month. There is also some extra cash to be made from side investments. However, at work, there are envious parties threaten to undermine or sabotage whatever good efforts you've put in. Do your best to resist any attempts by such malicious people to provoke you into an argument or dispute, which will only obscure all the good work you've done so far.

農曆七月 (August 7th - September 6th) 甲申

Those using this room may want to consider using another room this month, as you could find yourself feeling anxious and disturbed staying in this room. Salaried employees will find it difficult to make money, as the going will be tough regardless of how much effort they put into their work. That aside, the affluent and wealthy will find life to be a breeze this month. So, make the most of this opportunity to prepare for the inevitable rainy day.

農曆八月 (September 7th - October 7th) 乙酉

Opportunities will present themselves this month resulting in an upturn in fortunes and an increased financial income. Those expecting to be promoted to positions of authority and high social status could find these desires being fulfilled this month. People using this sector may be more inclined towards spiritual and religious pursuits.

農曆九月 (October 8th - November 6th) 丙戌

Use your wisdom and knowledge to reap the benefits due to you in the months to come while investing in real estate and property this month. The energies are favourable for self-improvement activities, so you could take the opportunity to do something you're interested in. Those engaged in the areas of media, advertising and writing will find this a good time of the year to produce as much revenue as possible from their efforts.

農曆十月 (November 7th - December 6th) 丁亥

Those of you involved in religious pursuits or gaining spiritual knowledge should use this bedroom, as the outcome is likely to be good. If you have a tendency towards mental instability, then it would be best to change bedrooms this month. This is a good month to make financial gains from the sale of property, but it will take its toll on your stress levels.

農曆十一月 (December 7th 2020 - January 4th 2021) 戊子

Couples who use this bedroom this month may find that their relationships are under severe stress that is likely to result in divorce. There is a chance of great fortune and financial gain but you will need to know what you are doing to realise these gains. Any business issues that arise this month should be dealt with after careful consideration or even after obtaining some help from lawyers.

農曆十二月 (January 5th - February 2nd 2021) 己丑

Where your health is concerned, take care of yourself and pay extra attention to your liver this month. Those of you who are in public relations will have to be prepared to face some unforeseen problems rearing their ugly heads. You will need to slow down, take stock of your situation, and plan your next move accordingly. If you're interested in starting your own business this month, or considering changing careers, then this is the month to do so. All activities of such nature are likely to be favourable and bring you good result.

農曆正月 (February 4th - March 4th) 戊寅

There is some extra cash to be made from side investments for those using this room. Medical professionals will find opportunities to leverage their status and income. However, you need to be mindful of jealous parties threatening to tarnish your reputation at work. Stay calm and avoid getting involved in an argument or dispute.

農曆二月 (March 5th - April 3rd) 己卯

Exercise tolerance and patience in all areas of your life as it will help to dispel any potential tension. Couples should be tolerant of each other and will need to put more effort into their relationships. Employers should be careful with labour relations this month as workers will challenge authority and become difficult to manage.

農曆三月 (April 4th - May 4th) 庚辰

Business owners must especially be careful of legal problems this month. There is a risk of endeavours meeting with failure this month so put on hold any grand plans for business expansion or to seek a promotion or even take on an ambitious project. Health-wise, watch out for stress-induced headaches and migraines.

農曆四月 (May 5th - June 4th) 辛巳

This should be a good month for those in the legal fields with strong demand for their skills, but you need to be careful of unwanted gossip. With the added complication of negative environmental forms, arguments could break out at work if the situation is not well-controlled. Diffuse the tension by refusing to join in the petty backbiting.

農曆五月 (June 5th - July 5th) 壬午

Politicians will find that they are able to promote their policies this month and end up with support from those around them. Business owners, however, should stay away from wheeling-dealing this month. Those who are employed should avoid changing jobs as well. There may be some tension between fathers and sons this time around.

農曆六月 (July 6th - August 6th) 癸未

If there are negative forms outside this sector, be careful of heart attacks or heart problems within this period. That aside, property investments will yield good gains this month and those in the real estate industry will also have a profitable month.

農曆七月 (August 7th - September 6th) 甲申

If you are looking to improve either your personal or professional relationships, you will find this a good month to do so. It also bodes well for travel in both leisure and business environment, especially if you are doing a fact-finding mission or are involved in research and development. Those in speculative investments or stocks and equities will make good profits this month if they use this bedroom.

農曆八月 (September 7th - October 7th) 乙酉

Parents of teenagers might find this a difficult month to deal with their children if they are using this sector. The elderly should take care of their health this month and see a doctor rather than dismiss minor ailments as insignificant. Be aware of travel-related problems this month that could result in injury to the limbs.

農曆九月 (October 8th - November 6th) 丙戌

This month, real estate developers will see opportunities to generate great wealth from their investments. Those who use this room are especially prone to head and brain issues, so consider moving away from this sector this month. Although there may be temptations this month, women should refrain from scandalous affairs.

農曆十月 (November 7th - December 6th) 丁亥

The skills and talents of those dabbling in the academic or legal field will be acknowledged and highly sought-after this month. However, there could be incessant power-struggles and jostling for authority amongst employees and management personnel in the workplace. Stay out of such a scenario if possible. Prioritise safety if you work with machinery on a regular or daily basis. You risk injuring yourself at work by neglecting this aspect.

農曆十一月 (December 7th 2020 - January 4th 2021) 戊子

The energies of this room will bode well for professional athletes participating in competitions and tournaments. Though, cut-throat competitions resulting in price wars may be expected this month. This seems to be a stressful and challenging month, but things will eventually sort themselves out as long as you're well-prepared.

農曆十二月 (January 5th - February 2nd 2021) 己丑

Miscommunication happens quite a bit easily this month. If you're negotiating deals, make sure you look through everything in black and white before you make agreements. You should be careful of your words at work, as at this point in time, misplaced words could cause you some cash – or worse yet, your job! If your relationship seems strained during this time, be tactful.

| Main Door | Northwest | Bedroom Sector | East |

SE | S | SW

6	2	4
5	**7**	9
1	3	8

E | | W

NE | N | NW

農曆正月 (February 4th - March 4th) 戊寅

Avoid engaging in speculative investments or even gambling this month, as these activities will likely result in heavy losses. Those using this room, however, will find mentors and superiors around to help you and offer some guidance and advice.

農曆二月 (March 5th - April 3rd) 己卯

Those who sleep in this bedroom will have to watch out for asthma attacks, bronchitis, rheumatism and joint problems. Singles will get to enjoy good Peach Blossom Luck, but the romantic prospects you find this month are likely to be short-lived flings. Lower your expectations to avoid disappointments later.

農曆三月 (April 4th - May 4th) 庚辰

Profits will experience a sharp decline so plan strategically for the future. Don't be overly disheartened if you find your business plagued by problems. Instead, persevere and see if you can get to the root of your problems. There will be a slowdown in the communications and entertainment industries this month. Mind your health as well to ward off the possibility of getting a skin disease or liver infection!

農曆四月 (May 5th - June 4th) 辛巳

Those in new relationships should ease off a little this month. Otherwise, they might find the romantic fires cooling off much sooner than expected. Stress and depression might worsen mental instability this month, especially if negative Sha is located in this sector. People in competitive sports will find competitions an uphill battle this month and should rather use the time to physically improve themselves.

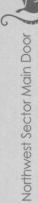

Main Door	Northwest	Bedroom Sector	East

農曆五月 (June 5th - July 5th) 壬午

Be mindful of disputes and acts of negligence, which could prove to be costly, especially to those dabbling in real estate and properties. Put any major personal endeavors on hold and wait until the right moment presents itself. This is not a good time for any important decision-making. Keep a close eye on your eldest daughter as well, as she's particularly susceptible to ill health due to the energies of the room this month.

農曆六月 (July 6th - August 6th) 癸未

If you have made profits from investments, it would be wise to cash in on these gains at this point in time. In addition, avoid gambling this month, as there is a strong possibility of losing property or even your entire fortune. Those in ill health should watch out for kidney problems, especially if cancer-related.

農曆七月 (August 7th - September 6th) 甲申

Manage your lifestyle carefully and seek a work-life balance in everything you do. You may be dismayed to find the stress and pressures of life taking their toll on your relationships this month. Look out as well for eye ailments and the possibility of suffering from a stroke if you happen to be using this bedroom.

農曆八月 (September 7th - October 7th) 乙酉

Mothers and older women who use this bedroom will find that their relationships are under strain this month. This is also not the time to start new ventures or businesses as the possibility of success is limited. However, those of you who are in the property and real estate fields and are in the know should be able to make quick, beneficial financial gains this month.

農曆九月 (October 8th - November 6th) 丙戌

Miscommunication is likely to happen this month. Lawyers and legal professionals will find it hard to put their cases across, as will those who rely on their vocal abilities for a livelihood such as motivational speakers. Don't worry unduly as this is only a temporary bad patch.

農曆十月 (November 7th - December 6th) 丁亥

The elderlies are particularly prone to head injuries and bone problems this month. It may hence be wise to have them undergo a full medical check-up if they happen to be using this bedroom. Avoid all investment deals this month. Chances are you'll only end up poorer than when you first started off by pouring your money into such ventures.

農曆十一月 (December 7th 2020 - January 4th 2021) 戊子

Business is likely to be slow and thus, this is not the time for any business expansion. Pay extra attention to customers and clients as disloyalty amongst employees is rife and this might affect your business in significant ways. Conservative property deals will bring financial gains this month but extreme caution needs to be exercised throughout the deals.

農曆十二月 (January 5th - February 2nd 2021) 己丑

For couples looking to conceive, this room will be ideal to use for the month. If you're involved in the academic and literary fields, you'll find this a good month for you in terms of increased inspiration and ideas. Go with your gut, and your head, and develop these new ideas well – as these are likely to bring about financial gains.

| Main Door | Northwest | Bedroom Sector | Northeast |

農曆正月 (February 4th - March 4th) 戊寅

This month your workplace responsibilities are likely to increase, making your schedule busier than usual. But worry not, as you will still have some personal time amidst your tight schedule for making future plans with your loved ones. Professional and personal relationships may be tainted by gossip and hearsay. You should stay above the fray to prevent things from getting out of hand.

農曆二月 (March 5th - April 3rd) 己卯

If negative features are found outside this sector, health problems could crop up this month, especially those who have diabetes or pregnant, and sleep in this bedroom. At work, there may well be some ulterior motives in play, especially for those who may have to contend with being bullied or pressured by colleagues at work.

農曆三月 (April 4th - May 4th) 庚辰

Tension enters into relationships, so extreme patience will be required throughout the month. Take extra care with present disputes as these may escalate into full legal problems. Look for overseas or offshore business opportunities in particular, as these are likely to enhance the bottom line.

農曆四月 (May 5th - June 4th) 辛巳

Married couples using this room are recommended to go on a holiday together at this time. Those who are in the entertainment industry or are running or employed in health centers, clubs and discos, as well as those sleeping in this bedroom will do well financially this month.

| Main Door | Northwest | Bedroom Sector | Northeast |

農曆五月 (June 5th - July 5th) 壬午

This is a good time to throw out the old and bring in the new as it is generally a month of improvements. Those in the creative industries will be in the limelight with a chance for you to make a name for yourself. Resist temptation leading you astray if you use this bedroom this month, as this may cause trouble with your present partner.

農曆六月 (July 6th - August 6th) 癸未

Business owners in the restaurant business or entertainment industry will see a boom this month. This is a month to ask for the promotion you wanted especially if you are in the food and beverage or media industries. In addition, there might also be a risk of heart and eye-related problems this particular time.

農曆七月 (August 7th - September 6th) 甲申

Those in the jewelry or jade business can expect good profits this month if they are using this bedroom. Business owners will make money and employees will experience career advancement, especially if they are in the oil and gas or the mining industries. Travelling brings positive benefits, including new investors into the business or open up new venture possibilities.

農曆八月 (September 7th - October 7th) 乙酉

Couples using this bedroom should be tolerant of each other this month as there is a risk of communications leading to conflicts. A month to avoid making important personal or financial decisions as you will find you are not able to make a clear one.

農曆九月 (October 8th - November 6th) 丙戌

Couples using this bedroom will be very lovey-dovey this month. However, if there is water outside this sector, be wary of extra-marital dalliances. Car accidents are also possible, so be careful on the road. That aside, this is a good month for those in the media business - there will be fame, recognition and some publicity.

農曆十月 (November 7th - December 6th) 丁亥

Pregnant women should avoid using this bedroom this month, as they may end up with complications or even a possible miscarriage. It will be difficult to make progress in anything this month so it would be best to take the back seat and consolidate your position. Turnover will be affected for those in the travel, courier and logistics businesses. Best to lie low and work through the challenging month.

農曆十一月 (December 7th 2020 - January 4th 2021) 戊子

Romance will bloom for those using this bedroom. Take advantage of this good time to seek out prospective partners if you are single. Asset acquisition will be successful this month, especially if it involves overseas travel. Engineering-related businesses will have a good month as media attention will bring in new customers.

農曆十二月 (January 5th - February 2nd 2021) 己丑

Speculative investments in property or equities, as well as stocks, will result in profits for you. However, you still need to be cautious when you proceed with making the deals. If you're a pregnant woman and using this room, you might run the risk of miscarriage if you don't pay special attention to your health. Other health problems that you could face include gastrointestinal ailments.

| Main Door | Northwest | Bedroom Sector | North |

農曆正月 (February 4th - March 4th) 戊寅

People involved in deals with overseas partners can make windfall gains this month. However, beware of fraud and theft, especially by close friends and family members. It would be advisable to put extra financial controls in place. People who are already in poor health should be careful of sustaining internal injuries.

農曆二月 (March 5th - April 3rd) 己卯

This is a good month for contractors to submit the tender for desired job as the outcome is likely to be positive. However, this is not a favourable month to travel for business as the journey will be plagued by problems throughout.

農曆三月 (April 4th - May 4th) 庚辰

Couples using this bedroom need to be more patient with each other to preserve harmony in their relationship. Legal issues arising from financial disputes or problems could well result in a loss of wealth this month if left unmonitored. Utilise your network of contacts to pave new ways for your business as such a step will bring about favorable results.

農曆四月 (May 5th - June 4th) 辛巳

Couples using this bedroom will find their relationship tense and strained this month. So exercise patience and tolerance with each other to minimize unnecessary friction. This is a good month to make that career move or embark on that new venture you've always wanted to do.

Main Door	Northwest	Bedroom Sector	North

農曆五月 (June 5th - July 5th) 壬午

Analysts and scientific researchers will benefit from the good energies of this room this month provided that there is a good quality mountain outside this sector. A lack of communication will cause problems in relationships, so endeavour to try and be more open with your partner. Personal safety should be made a priority this month, as there is a chance of being robbed and mugged.

農曆六月 (July 6th - August 6th) 癸未

Illnesses affecting the stomach and intestines will be a significant problem this month. Those who trade at markets or manage restaurants will find this to be a financially rewarding month. If you have outstanding fines or taxes owing, you may be in trouble with the law and should pay all outstanding penalties as soon as possible.

農曆七月 (August 7th - September 6th) 甲申

This is a favourable month for those in the construction industry especially if you are required to travel to conclude deals. Those artistically inclined, especially sculptors and carvers, will find that they attract increased commissions for their work. Mentors and counsellors will find that they are inundated by new clients looking for help and support.

農曆八月 (September 7th - October 7th) 乙酉

Good news will come to those who use this bedroom so long as they are involved in travel. During this period of time, you will likely have the chance to showcase your skills, so you are suggested to carry out your job to the best of your abilities. Let the quality of your work speak for itself, and you are likely to receive the recognition that you deserve.

農曆九月 (October 8th - November 6th) 丙戌

If there are negative features outside this room, prepare for the likelihood of health problems cropping up in the form of kidney trouble. Merchant bankers and equity dealers will find that they close better deals than usual, resulting in increased turnover and better profits.

農曆十月 (November 7th - December 6th) 丁亥

There will be good financial prospects for professionals in the literary, arts and other creative fields with your newfound fame and enhanced reputation contributing to your wealth luck. Avoid travelling this month, as your journeys will tend to be problematic.

農曆十一月 (December 7th 2020 - January 4th 2021) 戊子

industries will be able to pave inroads into markets traditionally dominated by their competitors this month. It would be wise to avoid unsavory spots and places of ill-repute especially this month, as your outings could result in arguments.

農曆十二月 (January 5th - February 2nd 2021) 己丑

If you're in the academic or literary field, this will be a good month for you in terms of getting funding, or attracting potential sponsors. However, health issues come to the forefront this month, so if you're suffering from any ailments affecting your internal organs especially the spleen, then take adequate care. Seek doctor's advice at the first sign of illness.

JOEY YAP's
QI MEN DUN JIA MASTERY PROGRAM

This is the world's most comprehensive training program on the subject of Qi Men Dun Jia. Joey Yap is the Qi Men Strategist for some of Asia's wealthiest tycoons. This program is modelled after Joey Yap's personal application methods, covering techniques and strategies he applies for his high net worth clients. There is a huge difference between studying the subject as a scholar and learning how to use it successfully as a Qi Men strategist. In this program, Joey Yap shares with you what he personally uses to transform his own life and the lives of million others. In other words, he shares with his students what actually works and not just what looks good in theory with no real practical value. This means that the program covers his personal trade secrets in using the art of Qi Men Dun Jia.

There are five unique programs, with each of them covering one specific application aspect of the Joey Yap's Qi Men Dun Jia system.

Joey Yap's training program focuses on getting results. Theories and formulas are provided in the course workbook so that valuable class time are not wasted dwelling on formulas. Each course comes with its own comprehensive 400-plus pages workbook. Taught once a year exclusively by Joey Yap, seats to these programs are extremely limited.

Getting Whatever You Want from Whatever You've Got™ Spiritual Qi Men™

Qi Men Forecasting Methods™

Qi Men Destiny & Life Transformation™

Qi Men Feng Shui™

Qi Men Strategic Execution™

Qi Men Warcraft™

Call +6(03) 2284 8080 or
email courses@masteryacademy.com for enquiries

JOEY YAP CONSULTING GROUP

Pioneering Metaphysics-Centric Personal and Corporate Consultations

Founded in 2002, the Joey Yap Consulting Group is the pioneer in the provision of metaphysics-driven coaching and consultation services for professionals and individuals alike. Under the leadership of the renowned international Chinese Metaphysics consultant, author and trainer, Dato' Joey Yap, it has become a world-class specialised metaphysics consulting firm with a strong presence in four continents, meeting the metaphysics-centric needs of its A-list clientele, ranging from celebrities to multinational corporations.

The Group's core consultation practice areas include Feng Shui, BaZi and Qi Men Dun Jia, which are complemented by ancillary services such as Date Selection, Face Reading and Yi Jing. Its team of highly trained professional consultants, led by its Chief Consultant, Dato' Joey Yap, is well-equipped with unparalleled knowledge and experience to help clients achieve their ultimate potentials in various fields and specialisations. Given its credentials, the Group is certainly the firm of choice across the globe for metaphysics-related consultations.

The Peerless Industry Expert

Benchmarked against the standards of top international consulting firms, our consultants work closely with our clients to achieve the best possible outcomes. The possibilities are infinite as our expertise extends from consultations related to the forces of nature under the subject of Feng Shui, to those related to Destiny Analysis and effective strategising under BaZi and Qi Men Dun Jia respectively.

To date, we have consulted a great diversity of clients, ranging from corporate clients – from various industries such as real estate, finance and telecommunication, amongst others – to the hundreds of thousands of individuals in their key life aspects. Adopting up-to-date and pragmatic approaches, we provide comprehensive services while upholding the importance of clients' priorities and effective outcomes. Recognised as the epitome of Chinese Metaphysics, we possess significant testimonies from worldwide clients as a trusted Brand.

Feng Shui Consultation

Residential Properties
- Initial Land/Property Assessment
- Residential Feng Shui Consultation
- Residential Land Selection
- End-to-End Residential Consultation

Commercial Properties
- Initial Land/Property Assessment
- Commercial Feng Shui Consultation
- Commercial Land Selection
- End-to-End Commercial Consultation

Property Developers
- End-to-End Consultation
- Post-Consultation Advisory Services
- Panel Feng Shui Consultant

Property Investors
- Your Personal Feng Shui Consultant
- Tailor-Made Packages

Memorial Parks & Burial Sites
- Yin House Feng Shui

BaZi Consultation

Personal Destiny Analysis
- Individual BaZi Analysis
- BaZi Analysis for Families

Strategic Analysis for Corporate Organizations
- BaZi Consultations for Corporations
- BaZi Analysis for Human Resource Management

Entrepreneurs and Business Owners
- BaZi Analysis for Entrepreneurs

Career Pursuits
- BaZi Career Analysis

Relationships
- Marriage and Compatibility Analysis
- Partnership Analysis

General Public
- Annual BaZi Forecast
- Your Personal BaZi Coach

Date Selection Consultation

- Marriage Date Selection
- Caesarean Birth Date Selection
- House-Moving Date Selection
- Renovation and Groundbreaking Dates
- Signing of Contracts
- O icial Openings
- Product Launches

Qi Men Dun Jia Consultation

Strategic Execution
- Business and Investment Prospects

Forecasting
- Wealth and Life Pursuits
- People and Environmental Matters

Feng Shui
- Residential Properties
- Commercial Properties

Speaking Engagement

Many reputable organisations and institutions have worked closely with Joey Yap Consulting Group to build a synergistic business relationship by engaging our team of consultants, which are led by Joey Yap, as speakers at their corporate events.

We tailor our seminars and talks to suit the anticipated or pertinent group of audience. Be it department subsidiary, your clients or even the entire corporation, we aim to fit your requirements in delivering the intended message(s) across.

CHINESE METAPHYSICS REFERENCE SERIES

The Chinese Metaphysics Reference Series is a collection of reference texts, source material, and educational textbooks to be used as supplementary guides by scholars, students, researchers, teachers and practitioners of Chinese Metaphysics.

These comprehensive and structured books provide fast, easy reference to aid in the study and practice of various Chinese Metaphysics subjects including Feng Shui, BaZi, Yi Jing, Zi Wei, Liu Ren, Ze Ri, Ta Yi, Qi Men Dun Jia and Mian Xiang.

The Chinese Metaphysics Compendium

At over 1,000 pages, the Chinese Metaphysics Compendium is a unique one-volume reference book that compiles ALL the formulas relating to Feng Shui, BaZi (Four Pillars of Destiny), Zi Wei (Purple Star Astrology), Yi Jing (I-Ching), Qi Men (Mystical Doorways), Ze Ri (Date Selection), Mian Xiang (Face Reading) and other sources of Chinese Metaphysics.

It is presented in the form of easy-to-read tables, diagrams and reference charts, all of which are compiled into one handy book. This first-of-its-kind compendium is presented in both English and its original Chinese language, so that none of the meanings and contexts of the technical terminologies are lost.

The only essential and comprehensive reference on Chinese Metaphysics, and an absolute must-have for all students, scholars, and practitioners of Chinese Metaphysics.

The Ten Thousand Year Calendar (Pocket Edition)

The Ten Thousand Year Calendar

Dong Gong Date Selection

The Date Selection Compendium

Plum Blossoms Divination Reference Book

Xuan Kong Da Gua Ten Thousand Year Calendar

San Yuan Dragon Gate Eight Formations Water Method

BaZi Hour Pillar Useful Gods - Wood

BaZi Hour Pillar Useful Gods - Fire

BaZi Hour Pillar Useful Gods - Earth

BaZi Hour Pillar Useful Gods - Metal

BaZi Hour Pillar Useful Gods - Water

Xuan Kong Da Gua Structures Reference Book

Xuan Kong Da Gua 64 Gua Transformation Analysis

BaZi Structures and Structural Useful Gods - Wood

BaZi Structures and Structural Useful Gods - Fire

BaZi Structures and Structural Useful Gods - Earth

BaZi Structures and Structural Useful Gods - Metal

BaZi Structures and Structural Useful Gods - Water

Earth Study Discern Truth Second Edition

Eight Mansions Bright Mirror

Secret of Xuan Kong

Ode to Flying Stars

Xuan Kong Purple White Script

Ode to Mysticism

The Yin House Handbook

Water Water Everywhere

Xuan Kong Da Gua Not Exactly For Dummies

Joey Yap's BaZi Profiling System

Three Levels of BaZi Profiling (English & Chinese versions)

In BaZi Profiling, there are three levels that reflect three different stages of a person's personal nature and character structure.

Level 1 – The Day Master

The Day Master in a nutshell is the basic you. The inborn personality. It is your essential character. It answers the basic question "who am I". There are ten basic personality profiles – the ten Day Masters – each with its unique set of personality traits, likes and dislikes.

Level 2 – The Structure

The Structure is your behavior and attitude – in other words, it is about how you use your personality. It expands on the Day Master (Level 1). The structure reveals your natural tendencies in life – are you a controller, creator, supporter, thinker or connector? Each of the Ten Day Masters express themselves differently through the five Structures. Why do we do the things we do? Why do we like the things we like? The answers are in our BaZi Structure.

Level 3 – The Profile

The Profile depicts your role in your life. There are ten roles (Ten BaZi Profiles) related to us. As to each to his or her own - the roles we play are different from one another and it is unique to each Profile.

What success means to you, for instance, differs from your friends – this is similar to your sense of achievement or whatever you think of your purpose in life is.

Through the BaZi Profile, you will learn the deeper level of your personality. It helps you become aware of your personal strengths and works as a trigger for you to make all the positive changes to be a better version of you.

Keep in mind, only through awareness that you will be able to maximise your natural talents, abilities and skills. Only then, ultimately, you will get to enter into what we refer as 'flow' of life – a state where you have the powerful force to naturally succeed in life.

www.BaZiprofiling.com

THE BaZi
60 PILLARS SERIES

The BaZi 60 Pillars Series is a collection of ten volumes focusing on each of the Pillars or Jia Zi in BaZi Astrology. Learn how to see BaZi Chart in a new light through the Pictorial Method of BaZi analysis and elevate your proficiency in BaZi studies through this new understanding. Joey Yap's 60 Pillars Life Analysis Method is a refined and enhanced technique that is based on the fundamentals set by the true masters of olden times, and modified to fit to the sophistication of current times.

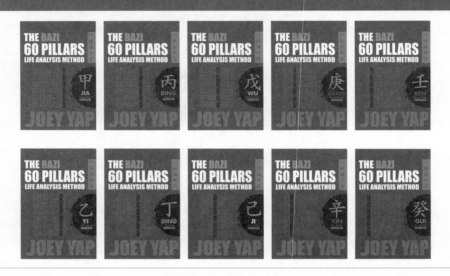

BaZi Collection

With these books, leading Chinese Astrology Master Trainer Joey Yap makes it easy to learn how to unlock your Destiny through your BaZi. BaZi or Four Pillars of Destiny is an ancient Chinese science which enables individuals to understand their personality, hidden talents and abilities, as well as their luck cycle - by examining the information contained within their birth data.

Understand and learn more about this accurate ancient science with this BaZi Collection.

| BOOK 1 | BOOK 2 | BOOK 3 | BOOK 4 | BOOK 5 | The 10 Gods |

(Available in English & Chinese)

Feng Shui Collection

Design Your Legacy

Design Your Legacy is Joey Yap's first book on the profound subject of Yin House Feng Shui, which is the study Feng Shui for burials and tombs. Although it is still pretty much a hidden practice that is largely unexplored by modern literature, the significance of Yin House Feng Shui has permeated through the centuries – from the creation of the imperial lineage of emperors in ancient times to the iconic leaders who founded modern China.

This book unveils the true essence of Yin House Feng Shui with its significant applications that are unlike the myths and superstition which have for years, overshadowed the genuine practice itself. Discover how Yin House Feng Shui – the true precursor to all modern Feng Shui practice, can be used to safeguard the future of your descendants and create a lasting legacy.

Must-Haves for Property Analysis!

For homeowners, those looking to build their own home or even investors who are looking to apply Feng Shui to their homes, these series of books provides valuable information from the classical Feng Shui therioes and applications.

In his trademark straight-to-the-point manner, Joey shares with you the Feng Shui do's and dont's when it comes to finding a property with favorable Feng Shui, which is condusive for home living.

Stories and Lessons on Feng Shui Series

All in all, this series is a delightful chronicle of Joey's articles, thoughts and vast experience - as a professional Feng Shui consultant and instructor - that have been purposely refined, edited and expanded upon to make for a light-hearted, interesting yet educational read. And with Feng Shui, BaZi, Mian Xiang and Yi Jing all thrown into this one dish, there's something for everyone.

(Available in English & Chinese)

More Titles under Joey Yap Books

Pure Feng Shui

Pure Feng Shui is Joey Yap's debut with an international publisher, CICO Books. It is a refreshing and elegant look at the intricacies of Classical Feng Shui - now compiled in a useful manner for modern day readers. This book is a comprehensive introduction to all the important precepts and techniques of Feng Shui practices.

Your Aquarium Here

This book is the first in Fengshuilogy Series, which is a series of matter-of-fact and useful Feng Shui books designed for the person who wants to do a fuss-free Feng Shui.

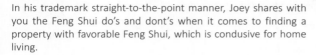

Walking the Dragons

Compiled in one book for the first time from Joey Yap's Feng Shui Mastery Excursion Series, the book highlights China's extensive, vibrant history with astute observations on the Feng Shui of important sites and places. Learn the landform formations of Yin Houses (tombs and burial places), as well as mountains, temples, castles and villages.

Walking the Dragons : Taiwan Excursion

A Guide to Classical Landform Feng Shui of Taiwan

From China to Tibet, Joey Yap turns his analytical eye towards Taiwan in this extensive Walking the Dragons series. Combined with beautiful images and detailed information about an island once known as Formosa, or "Beautiful Island" in Portuguese, this compelling series of essays highlights the colourful history and wonders of Taiwan. It also provides readers with fascinating insights into the living science of Feng Shui.

The Art of Date Selection: Personal Date Selection (Available in English & Chinese)

With the Art of Date Selection: Personal Date Selection, you can learn simple, practical methods to select not just good dates, but personalised good dates as well. Whether it is a personal activity such as a marriage or professional endeavour, such as launching a business - signing a contract or even acquiring assets, this book will show you how to pick the good dates and tailor them to suit the activity in question, and to avoid the negative ones too!

Your Head Here

Your Head Here is the first book by Sherwin Ng. She is an accomplished student of Joey Yap, and an experienced Feng Shui consultant and instructor with Joey Yap Consulting Group and Mastery Academy respectively. It is the second book under the Fengshuilogy series, which focuses on Bedroom Feng Shui, a specific topic dedicated to optimum bed location and placement.

If the Shoe Fits

This book is for those who want to make the effort to enhance their relationship.

In her debut release, Jessie Lee humbly shares with you the classical BaZi method of the Ten Day Masters and the combination of a new profiling system developed by Joey Yap, to understand and deal with the people around you.

Being Happy and Successful at Work and in your Career

Have you ever wondered why some of us are so successful in our careers while others are dragging their feet to work or switching from one job to another? Janet Yung hopes to answer this question by helping others through the knowledge and application of BaZi and Chinese Astrology. In her debut release, she shares with the readers the right way of using BaZi to understand themselves: their inborn talents, motivations, skills, and passions, to find their own place in the path of professional development.

Being Happy & Successful - Managing Yourself & Others

Manage Your Talent & Have Effective Relationships at the Workplace

While many strive for efficiency in the workplace, it is vital to know how to utilize your talents. In this book, Janet Yung will take you further on how to use the BaZi profiling system as a tool to assess your personality and understanding your approach to the job. From ways in communicating with your colleagues to understanding your boss, you will be astounded by what this ancient system can reveal about you and the people in your life. Tips and guidance will also be given in this book so that you will make better decisions for your next step in advancing in your career.

The BaZi Road to Success

The BaZi Road to Success explains your journey in life through a chart that is obtained just from looking at the date you were born and its connection with key BaZi elements.

Your Day Pillar, Hour Pillar, Luck Pillar and Annual Pillar all come together to paint a BaZi chart that churns out a combination of different elements, which the book helps interpret. From relationships, career advice, future plans and possibility of wealth accumulation - this book covers it all!

Face Reading Collection

The Chinese Art of Face Reading: The Book of Moles

The Book of Moles by Joey Yap delves into the inner meanings of moles and what they reveal about the personality and destiny of an individual. Complemented by fascinating illustrations and Joey Yap's easy-to-understand commentaries and guides, this book takes a deeper focus into a Face Reading subject, which can be used for everyday decisions – from personal relationships to professional dealings and many others.

Discover Face Reading (Available in English & Chinese)

This is a comprehensive book on all areas of Face Reading, covering some of the most important facial features, including the forehead, mouth, ears and even philtrum above your lips. This book will help you analyse not just your Destiny but also help you achieve your full potential and achieve life fulfillment.

Joey Yap's Art of Face Reading

The Art of Face Reading is Joey Yap's second effort with CICO Books, and it takes a lighter, more practical approach to Face Reading. This book does not focus on the individual features as it does on reading the entire face. It is about identifying common personality types and characters.

Faces of Fortune 2

We don't need to go far to look for entrepreneurs with the X-Factor. Malaysia produces some of the best entrepreneurs in the world. In this book, we will tell you the rags -to-riches stories of 9 ordinary people who has no special privileges, and how they made it on their own.

Easy Guide on Face Reading (Available in English & Chinese)

The Face Reading Essentials series of books comprises of five individual books on the key features of the face – the Eyes, the Eyebrows, the Ears, the Nose, and the Mouth. Each book provides a detailed illustration and a simple yet descriptive explanation on the individual types of the features.

The books are equally useful and effective for beginners, enthusiasts and those who are curious. The series is designed to enable people who are new to Face Reading to make the most out of first impressions and learn to apply Face Reading skills to understand the personality and character of their friends, family, co-workers and business associates.

2020 Annual Releases

Chinese Astrology for 2020 | Feng Shui for 2020 | Tong Shu Desktop Calendar 2020 | Daily Wall Calendar 2020 | Professional Tong Shu Diary 2020 | Tong Shu Monthly Planner 2020 | Weekly Tong Shu Diary 2020

Discover the True Significance of the Ancient Art of Lion Dance

The Lion has long been a symbol of power and strength. That powerful symbol has evolved into an incredible display of a mixture of martial arts and ritualism that is the Lion Dance. Throughout ancient and modern times, the Lion Dance has stamped itself as a popular part of culture, but is there a meaning lost behind this magnificent spectacle?

The Art of Lion Dance written by the world's number one man in Chinese Metaphysics, Dato' Joey Yap, explains the history and origins of the art and its connection to Qi Men Dun Jia. By creating that bridge with Qi Men, the Lion Dance is able to ritualise any type of ceremony, celebrations and mourning alike.

The book is the perfect companion to the modern interpretation of the art as it reveals the significance behind each part of the Lion costume, as well as rituals that are put in place to bring the costume and its spectacle to life.

Chinese Traditions & Practices

China has a long, rich history spanning centuries. As Chinese culture has evolved over the centuries, so have the country's many customs and traditions. Today, there's a Chinese custom for just about every important event in a person's life -- from cradle to the grave.

Although many China's customs have survived to the present day, some have been all but forgotten: rendered obsolete by modern day technology. This book explores the history of Chinese traditions and cultural practices, their purpose, and the differences between the traditions of the past and their modern incarnations.

If you are a westerner or less informed about Chinese culture, you may find this book particularly useful, especially when it comes to doing business with the Chinese — whether it be in China itself or some other country with a considerable Chinese population. If anything, it will allow you to have a better casual understanding of the culture and traditions of your Chinese friends or acquaintances. An understanding of Chinese traditions leads to a more informed, richer appreciation of Chinese culture and China itself.

Educational Tools and Software

Joey Yap's Feng Shui Template Set

Directions are the cornerstone of any successful Feng Shui audit or application. The Joey Yap Feng Shui Template Set is a set of three templates to simplify the process of taking directions and determining locations and positions, whether it is for a building, a house, or an open area such as a plot of land - all of it done with just a floor plan or area map.

The Set comprises three basic templates: The Basic Feng Shui Template, Eight Mansions Feng Shui Template, and the Flying Stars Feng Shui Template.

Mini Feng Shui Compass

The Mini Feng Shui Compass is a self-aligning compass that is not only light at 100gms but also built sturdily to ensure it will be convenient to use anywhere. The rings on the Mini Feng Shui Compass are bilingual and incorporate the 24 Mountain Rings that is used in your traditional Luo Pan.

The comprehensive booklet included with this, will guide you in applying the 24 Mountain Directions on your Mini Feng Shui Compass effectively and the Eight Mansions Feng Shui to locate the most auspicious locations within your home, office and surroundings. You can also use the Mini Feng Shui Compass when measuring the direction of your property for the purpose of applying Flying Stars Feng Shui.

MASTERY ACADEMY
OF CHINESE METAPHYSICS
Your **Preferred** Choice to the Art & Science of Classical Chinese Metaphysics Studies

Bringing **innovative** techniques and **creative** teaching methods to an ancient study.

Mastery Academy of Chinese Metaphysics was established by Joey Yap to play the role of disseminating this Eastern knowledge to the modern world with the belief that this valuable knowledge should be accessible to everyone and everywhere.

Its goal is to enrich people's lives through accurate, professional teaching and practice of Chinese Metaphysics knowledge globally. It is the first academic institution of its kind in the world to adopt the tradition of Western institutions of higher learning - where students are encouraged to explore, question and challenge themselves, as well as to respect different fields and branches of studies. This is done together with the appreciation and respect of classical ideas and applications that have stood the test of time.

The Art and Science of Chinese Metaphysics – be it Feng Shui, BaZi (Astrology), Qi Men Dun Jia, Mian Xiang (Face Reading), ZeRi (Date Selection) or Yi Jing – is no longer a field shrouded with mystery and superstition. In light of new technology, fresher interpretations and innovative methods, as well as modern teaching tools like the Internet, interactive learning, e-learning and distance learning, anyone from virtually any corner of the globe, who is keen to master these disciplines can do so with ease and confidence under the guidance and support of the Academy.

It has indeed proven to be a centre of educational excellence for thousands of students from over thirty countries across the world; many of whom have moved on to practice classical Chinese Metaphysics professionally in their home countries.

At the Academy, we believe in enriching people's lives by empowering their destinies through the disciplines of Chinese Metaphysics. Learning is not an option - it is a way of life!

MASTERY ACADEMY
OF CHINESE METAPHYSICS™

MALAYSIA
19-3, The Boulevard, Mid Valley City, 59200 Kuala Lumpur, Malaysia
Tel : +6(03)-2284 8080 | Fax : +6(03)-2284 1218
Email   : info@masteryacademy.com
Website   : www.masteryacademy.com

Australia, Austria, Canada, China, Croatia, Cyprus, Czech Republic, Denmark, France, Germany, Greece, Hungary, India, Italy, Kazakhstan, Malaysia, Netherlands (Holland), New Zealand, Philippines, Poland, Russian Federation, Singapore, Slovenia, South Africa, Switzerland, Turkey, United States of America, Ukraine, United Kingdom

The Mastery Academy around the world!

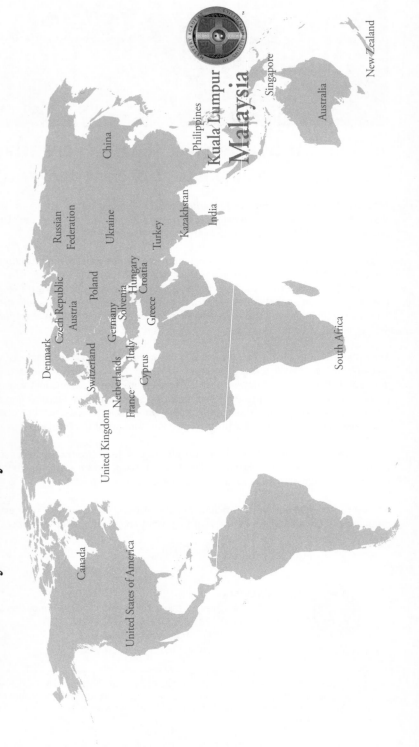

United States of America
Canada

United Kingdom

Denmark
Czech Republic
Austria
Switzerland
Poland
Netherlands
Germany
France
Italy
Slovenia
Hungary
Croatia
Cyprus
Greece

Russian Federation

Ukraine

Turkey

Kazakhstan

India

South Africa

China

Philippines
Kuala Lumpur
Malaysia

Singapore
Australia

New Zealand

Feng Shui Mastery™
LIVE COURSES (MODULES ONE TO FOUR)

This an ideal program for those who wants to achieve mastery in Feng Shui from the comfort of their homes. This comprehensive program covers the foundation up to the advanced practitioner levels, touching upon the important theories from various classical Feng Shui systems including Ba Zhai, San Yuan, San He and Xuan Kong.

Module One:
Beginners
Course

Module Two:
Practitioners
Course

Module Three:
Advanced
Practitioners Course

Module Four:
Master Course

BaZi Mastery™
LIVE COURSES (MODULES ONE TO FOUR)

This lesson-based program brings a thorough introduction to BaZi and guides the student step-by-step, all the way to the professional practitioner level. From the theories to the practical, BaZi students along with serious Feng Shui practitioners, can master its application with accuracy and confidence.

Module One:
Intensive
Foundation Course

Module Two:
Practitioners
Course

Module Three:
Advanced
Practitioners Course

Module Four:
Master Course in BaZi

Xuan Kong Mastery™
LIVE COURSES (MODULES ONE TO THREE)
* Advanced Courses For Master Practitioners

Xuan Kong is a sophisticated branch of Feng Shui, replete with many techniques and formulae, which encompass numerology, symbology and the science of the Ba Gua, along with the mathematics of time. This program is ideal for practitioners looking to bring their practice to a more in-depth level.

Module One:
Advanced
Foundation Course

Module Two A:
Advanced Xuan
Kong Methodologies

Module Two B:
Purple White

Module Three:
Advanced Xuan Kong
Da Gua

Mian Xiang Mastery™
LIVE COURSES (MODULES ONE AND TWO)

This program comprises of two modules, each carefully developed to allow students to familiarise with the fundamentals of Mian Xiang or Face Reading and the intricacies of its theories and principles. With lessons guided by video lectures, presentations and notes, students are able to understand and practice Mian Xiang with greater depth.

Module One:
Basic Face
Reading

Module Two:
Practical Face
Reading

Yi Jing Mastery™
LIVE COURSES (MODULES ONE AND TWO)

Whether you are a casual or serious Yi Jing enthusiast, this lesson-based program contains two modules that brings students deeper into the Chinese science of divination. The lessons will guide students on the mastery of its sophisticated formulas and calculations to derive answers to questions we pose.

Module One:
Traditional Yi Jing

Module Two:
Plum Blossom
Numerology

Ze Ri Mastery™
LIVE COURSES (MODULES ONE AND TWO)

In two modules, students will undergo a thorough instruction on the fundamentals of ZeRi or Date Selection. The comprehensive program covers Date Selection for both Personal and Feng Shui purposes to Xuan Kong Da Gua Date Selection.

Module One:
Personal and
Feng Shui Date
Selection

Module Two:
Xuan Kong
Da Gua Date
Selection

Joey Yap's
SAN YUAN QI MEN XUAN KONG DA GUA™

This is an advanced level program which can be summed up as the Integral Vision of San Yuan studies – an integration of the ancient potent discipline of Qi Men Dun Jia and the highly popular Xuan Kong 64 Hexagrams. Often regarded as two independent systems, San Yuan Qi Men and San Yuan Xuan Kong Da Gua can trace their origins to the same source and were actually used together in ancient times by great Chinese sages.

This method enables practitioners to harness the Qi of time and space, and predict the outcomes through a highly-detailed analysis of landforms, places and sites.

BaZi 10X

Emphasising on the practical aspects of BaZi, this programme is rich with numerous applications and techniques pertaining to the pursuit of wealth, health, relationship and career, all of which constitute the formula of success. This programme is designed for all levels of practitioners and is supplemented with innovative learning materials to enable easy learning. Discover the different layers of BaZi from a brand new perspective with BaZi 10X.

Feng Shui for Life

This is an entry-level five-day course designed for the Feng Shui beginner to learn the application of practical Feng Shui in day-to-day living. Lessons include quick tips on analysing the BaZi chart, simple Feng Shui solutions for the home, basic Date Selection, useful Face Reading techniques and practical Water formulas. A great introduction course on Chinese Metaphysics studies for beginners.

Joey Yap's
Design Your Destiny

This is a three-day life transformation program designed to inspire awareness and action for you to create a better quality of life. It introduces the DRT™ (Decision Referential Technology) method, which utilises the BaZi Personality Profiling system to determine the right version of you, and serves as a tool to help you make better decisions and achieve a better life in the least resistant way possible, based on your Personality Profile Type.

Millionaire Feng Shui Secrets Programme

This program is geared towards maximising your financial goals and dreams through the use of Feng Shui. Focusing mainly on the execution of Wealth Feng Shui techniques such as Luo Shu sectors and more, it is perfect for boosting careers, businesses and investment opportunities.

Grow Rich With BaZi Programme

This comprehensive programme covers the foundation of BaZi studies and presents information from the career, wealth and business standpoint. This course is ideal for those who want to maximise their wealth potential and live the life they deserve. Knowledge gained in this course will be used as driving factors to encourage personal development towards a better future.

Walk the Mountains!
Learn Feng Shui in a Practical and Hands-on Program

 ### Feng Shui Mastery Excursion™

Learn landform (Luan Tou) Feng Shui by walking the mountains and chasing the Dragon's vein in China. This program takes the students in a study tour to examine notable Feng Shui landmarks, mountains, hills, valleys, ancient palaces, famous mansions, houses and tombs in China. The excursion is a practical hands-on course where students are shown to perform readings using the formulas they have learnt and to recognise and read Feng Shui Landform (Luan Tou) formations.

Read about the China Excursion here:
http://www.fengshuiexcursion.com

Mastery Academy courses are conducted around the world. Find out when will Joey Yap be in your area by visiting
www.masteryacademy.com
or call our offices at **+6(03)-2284 8080**.